W9-BNV-260

ANDREW
JENKS
MY ADVENTURES AS
A YOUNG FILMMAKER

GTO
NEVADA
68 GTO
DREAM CAR RENTALS

ANDREW JENKS

MY ADVENTURES AS A YOUNG FILMMAKER

SCHOLASTIC INC.

Cover: Main photo: Brad Jones; Andrew Siegel; Paul Birman; Mike Sierakowski; Jonah Quickmire Pettigrew

Pages 20–21: *Manneken Pis*: © Ronald Sumners/Shutterstock; *Belgian flag*: © Jim Barber/Shutterstock; pages 22–23: *Brussels Grand Place*: © CRM/Shutterstock; page 26: *Old fan*: iStockphoto; *Outdoor fan*: iStockphoto; page 34: *Andrew playing basketball*: Chase Media Group. © 2003 All rights reserved.; page 36: *Budding Spielberg*: From *The Journal News*, May 15 © 2003 *The Journal News*. All rights reserved. Used by permission and protected by the Copyright Laws of the United States. The printing, copying, redistribution, or retransmission of this Content without express written permission is prohibited.; *Film buff*: © North County News; page 81: *Premiere*: © Stephen Lovekin/Getty Images; page 96: *Room 335*: © *Variety*; page 97: *From college dorm to nursing home*: From *The Journal News*, January 13 © 2008 *The Journal News*. All rights reserved. Used by permission and protected by the Copyright Laws of the United States. The printing, copying, redistribution, or retransmission of this Content without express written permission is prohibited.; *Youthful filmmaker*: © *Daily News*, L.P. (New York); page 110: *Bobby V. in costume*: © MLB.com; pages 150–151: *Q&A*: © Scott Wintrow/Getty Images for Tribeca Film Festival; page 153: *Andrew on WNYC Radio*: © Jody Avirgan/WNYC Radio; *Andrew at Tribeca Film Festival*: © Bryan Bedder/Getty Images for Tribeca Film Festival; *Promoting*: © Andrew Marks/Corbis; page 193: *College speaking*: © Chris Neverman; pages 208–209: *MTV filmmaker visits SCSU*: © Nick Simmons/*University Chronicle*; *At JMU*: © *The Breeze*; *At Columbia college*: © Ashley Osborn.

The publisher wishes to thank the following for use of their photos.
Akshay Bhansali, Paul Birman, Bruce Bohman (especially for those movie posters), ESPN, Will Godel, Jonathan Jaeger, Jenks family, Brad Jones, Brian Lindenbaum, Chris Lopez, MTV, Andrew Muscato, Tom Oliva, Jonah Quickmire Pettigrew, Phoenix Film Festival, Luca Repola, Andrew Siegel, Mike Sierakowski, Kassie Thornton Bobby Valentine, Daniel Zinn

Library of Congress Cataloging-in-Publication Data Available

ISBN 978-0-545-41727-3

10 9 8 7 6 5 4 3 2 1 13 14 15 16 17/0

Printed in China 38
First printing, March 2013
Book design by Rick DeMonico

Contents

Introduction

A few people are calling me.

Where did he go?

I get a voice mail from my mom: "Andrew, aren't you at the VMAs? Thought you flew there. Maybe I am confused. I forget what city you're in. Dad can't remember either. Anyway, call us tomorrow; we're heading to bed."

I just locked myself inside a bathroom at the VMAs. And I don't want to get out. MTV's Video Music Awards, which ten million people are currently watching, is airing. And inside the bathroom, I can hear the loud noises only a few feet away. The premiere of my show airs directly after.

I've just been on the red carpet with the world's biggest stars. Lady Gaga. Justin Bieber. Kanye West. A publicist directed me toward the top of the red carpet, where I did a live interview on MTV.

During the opening of the awards, I sat in awe as Eminem performed, and when he was done, I checked my e-mail. We're still in the middle of editing my new show, and I'd just gotten the latest cut of an episode we'd been working on for months. I decided to go to the bathroom. You just can't top Eminem—and it was more productive to do some work. I thought nobody would notice I'd gone other than the seat filler who took my seat.

Now, in the bathroom, I'm watching on my phone. Pausing every few minutes to take notes. My leg shakes uncontrollably—it usually does. As I sit on the toilet, I watch my eight days living on the streets of San Francisco with a homeless young woman. I want to see how the show has developed before

I head to a Dallas prison to do an interview for an entirely different episode. The show is getting better, but there is still work to be done.

My phone rings. I pick it up.

It's J.J. Hill, who's been one of my best friends since elementary school. We talk a lot.

"Yo, Jenks."

"What's up, man?"

"Why are you whispering?"

"I am working in the bathroom."

"What are you working on in the bathroom?"

"I feel like the show needs work. I am just working on it in here. It's easier."

J.J. knows me too well to question what I am doing. So he just continues…

"You want to play ball tomorrow? I got a good group of guys to play."

"I am in Los Angeles, man. At the VMAs."

J.J.'s forgotten. Typical. I've had the same group of friends my whole life. They are everything to me. And they couldn't care less about the VMAs. In fact, most of them have never attended any one of my movie premieres. But if I ever told them I needed their help—they would drop everything and run.

In this case, J.J. just wants me to play basketball.

"Well, call me when you get back tomorrow. I am telling you, it's going to be a great pickup game."

I put down my phone and look around.

I am 23 years old. How did I get here?

Why is the awkward kid who went through puberty way too early and pretended he was a filmmaker by practicing his Oscar speech in the mirror now at the hottest show on the planet?

I've had some wonderful experiences:

- I moved into a nursing home when I was 19 and made a movie about it that sold to HBO.
- I dropped out of college and moved to Japan to make a movie for ESPN.
- I created and starred in my own MTV show.

Of course, there's more to it. A lot more.

There is not just the wild, outlandish, risky, and sometimes lavish journey I have been on, but above all, there is the story of the work: shooting tens of thousands of hours of footage; late nights focusing to the point of forgetting an outside world exists; crying over the ones I've lost; recovering from trying to absorb the worlds I'm forced to leave; having people ground me, give me their time, pick me up when I think it's all over, and take a big chance on me; feeling guilty and angry for not doing the right thing; and feeling proud of what I have done.

That night in Beverly Hills, I went to bed as five million people watched my show and I started to trend on Twitter worldwide. As I was falling asleep, J.J. calls.

"I am telling you, this is going to be an amazing game."

"I know, man. I am taking the first flight back."

chapter one

BLOW THIS THING UP

In the middle of Washington Square Park on a cold winter day

Thursday nights in the dorm were always brutal.

The *O.C.* theme song started ringing through the hallways at ten P.M. By eleven, you heard bottles opening. By midnight, you heard them crashing. At one A.M., things started to smell odd. By two, there was yelling from the street. And at three in the morning, another kind of yelling.

Through it all, I sat at my laptop, staring at a nun making the best sex joke I'd heard in years, trying to match her words with the video. It wasn't in sync. Nothing was working.

I was in my first year of film school at New York University, the best film school in the best city in the world. The hallways and rooms, lined with Martin Scorsese and Spike Lee posters, had a lot of history. Everyone walked with a certain swagger. My dorm was on Washington Square West, a loud, lively, artistic, near-perfect part of the city.

But I was completely miserable. Everything was hopeless—making friends, becoming a filmmaker, even going to class. I hadn't shown up for one of those in a while.

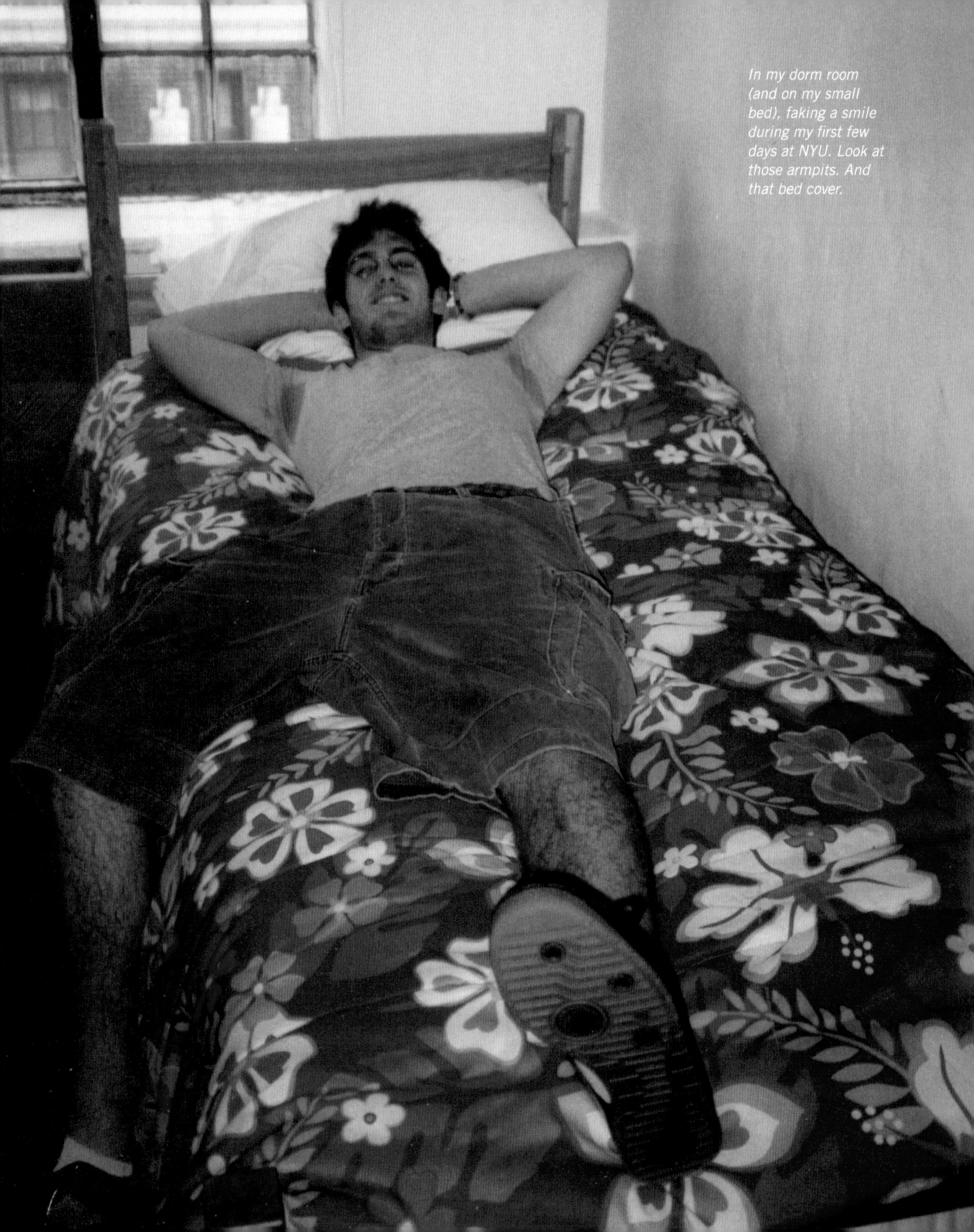

In my dorm room (and on my small bed), faking a smile during my first few days at NYU. Look at those armpits. And that bed cover.

I did not get the other kids. The most popular guy was an actor who'd had a bit part in *Mean Girls*, and that's all he would talk about—how funny Tina Fey was on set or what it was like to be in the same car with Lindsay Lohan (I know because, of course, I was in every class with him). Everyone was so geeked out about it and couldn't get enough of his endless stories. That's what college was about: being a star, or at least being near one.

Meanwhile, I wanted to disappear. Every night around one A.M., I ate at a tiny sandwich place with a guy who' d lived on MacDougal for the last thirty years. I can still remember the leather jacket he wore every night, his cigarettes, his raspy voice. He'd tell me how he used to eat sandwiches on the same street with Bob Dylan and Jimi Hendrix and a bunch of other celebrities back in their prime.

Now we both sat. Him thinking about what once was. Me thinking about how the heck I ended up here.

Night after night, I returned to my dorm room to work on a trailer about a group of residents at a senior citizen home that I'd shot the summer before freshman year. I tuned out the sounds of Lower Manhattan and buried myself in their images—drooping eyelids, decaying or too-white teeth—and their wise and funny jokes, like those of the nun asking if I'd heard the one about the eighty-year-old husband who couldn't get it up with his wife anymore. But I had screwed up the trailer; the sound didn't match the picture, a common mistake for anyone who is editing and learning at the same time. Trying to piece the audio tracks back with the visuals was driving me so completely insane that my leg started to shake uncontrollably.

I was just about to bang my fist on the desk when my roommate opened the door.

"Dude," he said. "Old people? Again?"

Looking back, it's not a surprise college was a bust. I never liked being away from home. Around third grade, when sleepovers were a big night out, I was horrified. Unable to fall asleep anywhere, except in my house and in my bed, I'd lie in the dark, staring at nothing, listening to my friends snoring, until I couldn't take another second. "Anyone still awake?" I asked. At one in the morning, I broke down and begged my mom over the phone to come get me. When high school rolled around, I wasn't any different. I guess the only difference is that I had the courage to stay the entire night. I wouldn't sleep. My heart would beat fast. But I knew I was too old to cry and go home.

My chronic homesickness has always been a strange fact. I spent a lot of time as a kid traveling, because my dad, Bruce (British accent, with a beard, Oxford PhD, and a brain most, including me, have issues keeping up with), worked for the United Nations. He moved our family to Nepal for a couple of years when I was six months old, which I don't remember (even though Nepali became my first language). And then, in 1995, when I was nine years old, we moved to Belgium.

Top: My dad in Tiananmen Square, Beijing—1991
Bottom left: My dad in Belgium, listening to an interpreter—1995
Bottom right: My dad with Prince Charles—2011

B. Jenks
H. Van Rompuy

From left to right: Taking one of my first pictures; our house in Nepal; with Mom, flying back home; relaxation time; posing with Mount Everest; playing balaphone; always on the go with Mom; with Dad

Welcome to Brussels, Belgium. Before I stepped off that plane I knew a few things about the place; the people speak French and Flemish, they're damn proud of their waffles (I would be, too), and one of their most famous landmarks is the Manneken Pis. My mom, younger brother, Matt, and I arrived in the morning and met my dad at the new house.

I was nine.

What am I doing here?

I walked up to my new room, crying. What the house looked like didn't matter. My mom felt bad but was tired herself. She did all she could; she gave me an electric fan (more on this later) and told me to get some sleep.

Instead I wrote a letter.

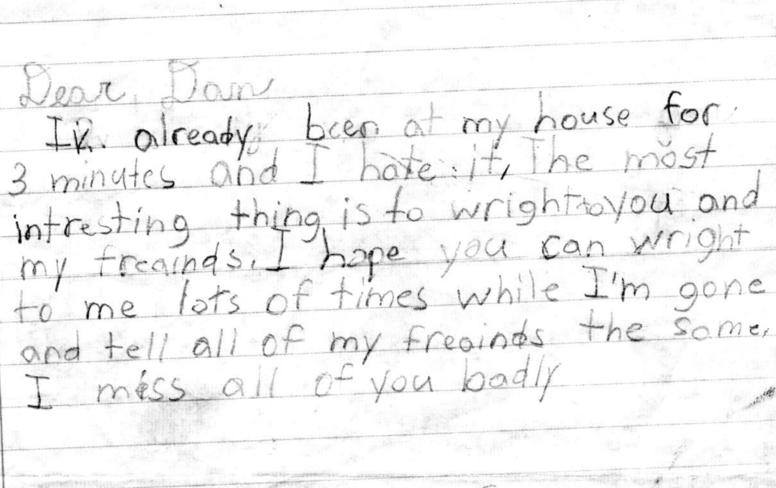

Dear, Dan

I'v already been at my house for 3 minutes and I hate it, The most intresting thing is to wright to you and my freainds. I hope you can wright to me lots of times while I'm gone and tell all of my freainds the same. I miss all of you badly

from
Aandrew

P.S.
It takes me 6 minutes to get a pencil.

BEST FRIENDS

Top: My best friend, Dan Zinn, and me during Halloween in our small town an hour north of New York City. Below: Our letter exchanges. Looks like I had issues spelling my name.

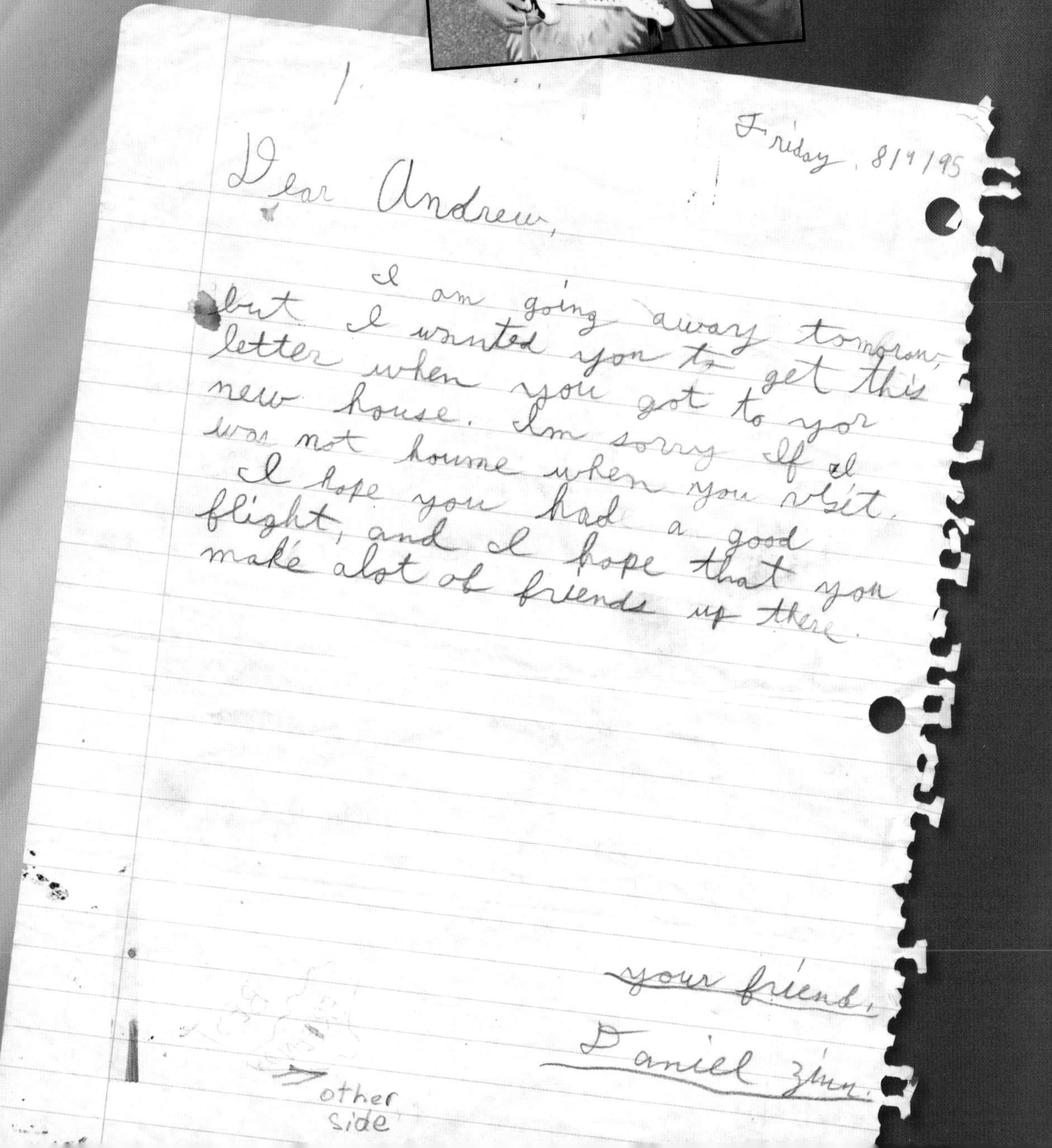

1

Friday, 8/4/95

Dear Andrew,

I am going away tomorow, but I wanted you to get this letter when you got to yor new house. Im sorry if I was not houme when you vset. I hope you had a good flight, and I hope that you make alot of friends up there.

your friend,

Daniel Zinn.

other side

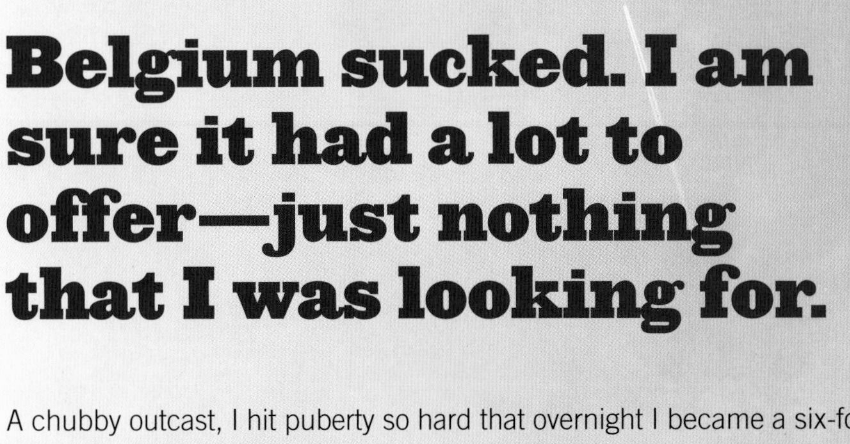

Belgium sucked. I am sure it had a lot to offer—just nothing that I was looking for.

A chubby outcast, I hit puberty so hard that overnight I became a six-foot-one fifth-grader with the voice of a middle-aged man. Instead of turning tall and suave, there was just more of me to feel awkward. I hadn't become a man but a huge baby. People called me the gentle giant.

I was very much by myself, except for my family and they didn't count (because at that age, even though I would cry if Mom wasn't around for one night, you still prefer the company of friends). Our weekend trips, when we packed into the Volvo and drove all around Europe, were no consolation. Luxembourg. Germany. Spain. You name it. My parents thought they were educating Matt and me by taking us to Greece to see the sites of the ancient Olympics. But I just wanted to go home. The world was too big.

The way I kept myself from going crazy was to parcel out time in increments that I knew I could get through. "In ten days we are going to be back in Belgium," I remember saying to my brother during a trip to Utrecht. "Once we get back to Belgium, then two weeks after that maybe we can play some basketball and then two weeks after that, we are going to be back in New York visiting friends."

Our travels in Europe

Basketball. My brother. Friends. Home.

I couldn't always have those things, but there were two things I never went anywhere without.

Since second grade, I have never slept without a fan blowing right into my face. When I don't have a fan, even when exhausted, **I just don't sleep.** I try. But I end up turning on the TV. Or lying for hours thinking. Thinking about how anxious I am to start the next project. Write the great script. Make the big film. But I lie there. And feel empty. I realize I need to breathe.

Relax. You're doing just fine.

Put that fan on, and all of those racing, harmful, continuous thoughts vanish. I have no idea why.

I remember each fan and from what time in my life I used it. Almost like the women I have dated, I have unique relationships with each and every one of them.

RE™
ROOM ESSENTIALS

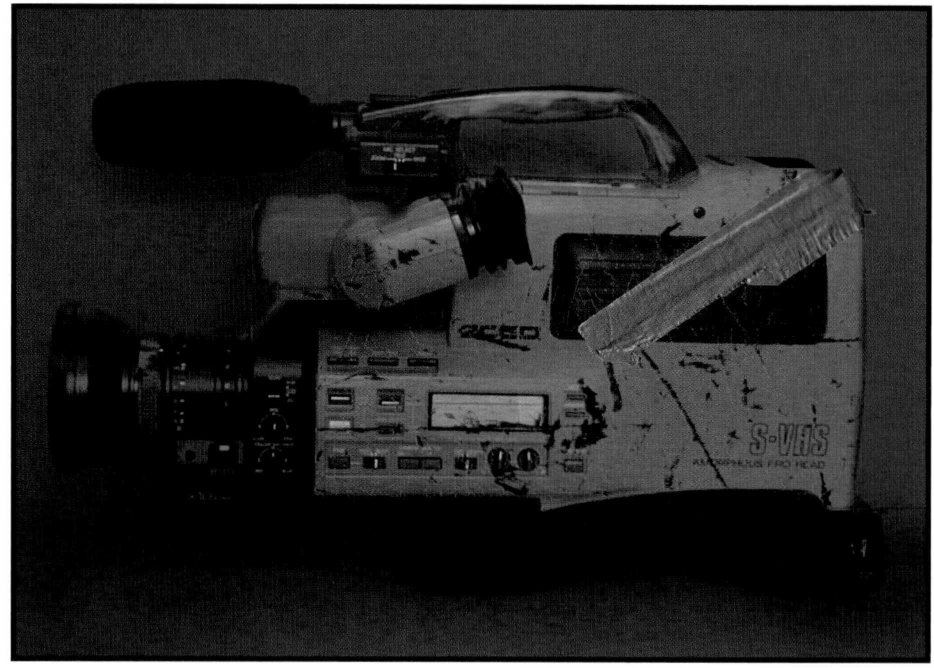

My best friend, the camera

In Brussels, if the fan was my security blanket at night, then the video camera was the same for daytime. Neither living nor breathing, it was mostly my companion. My mom, Nancy, had bought the camera because she wanted to send tapes of us back to my grandparents in the States. In Belgium, without anything to do—I wasn't into reading, the Internet wasn't a thing yet, and *Saved by the Bell* only played at 6:30 P.M. in Flemish—**I started using the camera by default.**

Other than my family, the only thing that consoled me was that big, bulky VHS camera, which I started taking with me everywhere I went. It didn't matter if nothing was going on, I still filmed it. Footage of grass with this narration: "Here's the grass growing. What's going to happen in three months?"

My camera meant action even in the most boring places. On one of our family trips to see something that looked like a hut in the middle of nowhere, I walked around all day, pretending to be a CNN correspondent. Through the lens, everything seemed a lot cooler. I filmed a crumbling wall as if I were reporting from just outside Jerusalem, while a dirt road was war-torn Somalia. "Bringing you the world," I said, mimicking the network's famous tagline voiced by James Earl Jones. "This is CNN." I started every video I shot during the two long years we lived in Belgium with that line. . . . "Bringing you the world."

Even though nobody saw the weather report I did on a drive through France or the *Mission: Impossible* miniseries I made, starring Matt Jenks, as far as I was concerned, the world was my audience. And my toughest critic, as always, was my brother. In Belgium, when shooting a scene for our latest short action film, I'd thought it'd be dramatic if I jumped off a couch and fell hard to the ground. I remember Matt saying, "A couch?" He was disgusted. "Let's go outside and jump off the roof. It'd look much cooler."

When finding images for this book, I went through hours of old footage—and I actually spent 30 minutes narrating the story of this grass.

Even though I returned to New York in sixth grade, I never gave up the camera. I continued to shoot video all the time, pretending to be blink-182 in my own music video or doing fake news reports with friends.

In high school, a couple of friends and I went public with our "news program." Public access, that is. On the local channel (nicely placed at channel six, in between Fox and ABC), featuring shows by anyone who was willing to make them, we called ours *Internal Injustice*, which made no sense but we thought the alliteration sounded good. *I.I.* was our own personal version of the *Today* show, with a mix of news, sports, weather, and cooking (in one episode, we taught viewers how to cook a hot dog).

I couldn't believe it. All I had to do was tape the show, edit it, and then drop off the tape at the local public access station. And boom, prime-time TV.

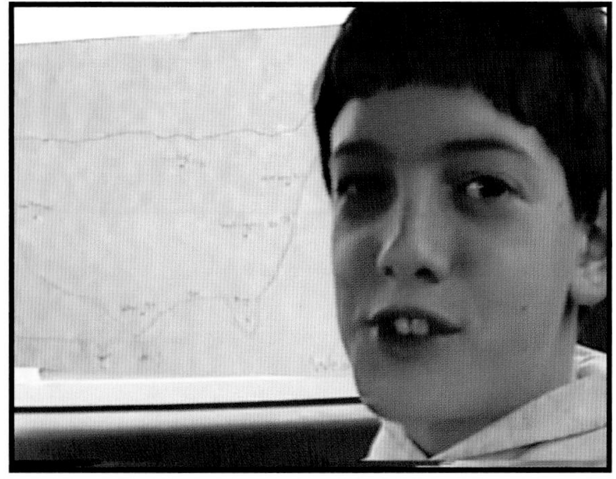

From left to right: Playing a local weather man, reporting from a "live earthquake" with my brother, performing in my own music video, acting as the evil villain in our own black-and-white movie

After the episode aired in which we ranked the top three pizza places in town (the perfect service journalism piece, in my opinion), I walked into the pizza spot that I went to every day for lunch because of its proximity to my high school—only to be refused service.

"If we weren't good enough to make your list, then I don't think you should eat here," one of the big Italian brothers told me after I tried to order a slice.

The guy was kicking me out of his pizza place, and I never felt cooler. *People are actually watching I.I.!* I tried to play it off like it was no big deal, but the pizza man wouldn't hear it.

"If you want to talk about it more, come back tomorrow and we'll talk in the parking lot," he said.

He cared enough to threaten me.

This was big. I headed straight from the pizza place to see Dan Zinn, one of my best friends and *I.I.* colleagues, and gave him my plan.

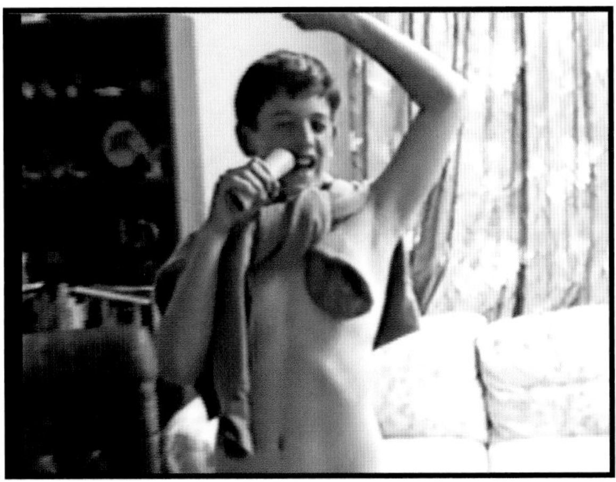

The next day I returned to the pizza place and told the guys, "I'd love to enjoy your pizza as I always do, but if you want to talk outside, let's talk outside." Zinn had gone to the restaurant a half hour beforehand and was sitting with a piece of pizza by the big picture window—a perfect spot to film the action in the parking lot. I followed the guy outside, holding a sweater in my hand that hid a small tape recorder.

"What's up?" I said loudly into my sweater.

"What's up?" The guy turned red. "What's up? I'm running a business. That's what's up. Who do you think you are, doing some show about how my pizza blows? I've got customers coming in saying I wasn't even rated on this thing. . . ." This was pure TV gold. I was a tenth-grade Mike Wallace. The guy went off while I secretly recorded him and my buddy got the visuals. Despite the verbal abuse, I didn't get a single scratch, which I was pretty conflicted about.

After editing our piece of strange, outlandish investigative journalism, we were pumped and ready to air the most explosive episode of *I.I.* yet. If the pizza ratings had made a stir, I couldn't imagine what this would elicit.

Too bad I never got to find out.

From left to right: Reporting on local and national news and sports, and a cooking segment on how to best cook a hot dog

"You can't air this," a manager of the public access station told us, returning our tape. "We'll get sued. Forget it."

We were disappointed but not deterred. In our search for cutting-edge material, we decided to do what I was calling the "Exclusive Interview with Max Ferber." Max was a friend of mine who had been busted for pot and suspended from school. In our thoughtful sit-down, he talked about how he'd made a mistake and wasn't going to do it again. But when the school—not to mention his parents—found out, that was it. Public Access and my school asked us to stop showing up with tapes for our Friday night slot. I guess, in so many words, we were canceled. *Internal Injustice* was too controversial. Exactly.

The first time I realized the full extent to which I enjoyed making movies was at the end-of-the-year party for our high school basketball team.

Now, my basketball team was much more than just some high school sport. Seven of the guys on it had been my best friends for my entire life. My parents sent me to a Jewish preschool, although I am not Jewish, and that's where I met: J.J. Hill (#3), Will Sprouse (#9), Keith Bielory (#15), Brian Kuritzky (#16), Dan Zinn (#17), Brian Lindenbaum (#20), and John Jaeger (#22).

They have my back, and I will always have theirs. We're a family. For our entire lives, we were an undersized, oftentimes overmatched squad. Nobody ever really minded playing the Sailors (yes, our real team name).

It seemed that almost every experience I had, one of these guys who made up my core group of friends was involved. In kindergarten, Lindenbaum and I started a business making construction-paper chains. We would sit in one of our houses and make fifty-yard chains that went all the way up and down the steps, which we sold for ten cents a link (these were high-quality chains linked together using glue, and not awful-looking staples). It was a booming business; we sold them to the gym teacher for the birthdays at school that seemed to happen once a week, and to other teachers to decorate the bulletin boards outside classrooms. Eventually word got around to the principal, who shut us down for committing commercial transactions during school hours.

Despite the things that came and went, like our paper-chain company, basketball was a constant. We were all on the Blue Mountain Middle School team. When we went to Hendrick Hudson High School, we played JV and then varsity. We were so obsessed that we played on a weekend Catholic League team. Although we made it to the playoffs every year, we were disqualified from competing because most of our team didn't go to church.

At Hen Hud, it was different; we were champs. So when the team asked me to put together a highlight reel of our best moments for the year-end celebration, I had a lot of material and decided to take it a step further. I made a cool ESPN-inspired piece complete with pop music and slow-mo effects. At the end, though, I departed from the form.

Looks like I'm about to get blocked.

Around the fourth minute of the film, the montage just stopped and suddenly there was J.J. (the best player on our team) playing one-on-one against Kyle Chewning. (The thirteenth man on the team, Kyle was the worst player but also the most energized. So whenever our team was in the paper, the article always featured a huge picture of Kyle pumping his fist or jumping high in the air even though he never had anything to do with the winning play.) Having missed some shots, J.J. finds himself only one basket away from losing to Kyle. Then J.J. trips and Kyle's about to go in for the winning shot when J.J.'s mother, Brenda, appears in the frame. Watching the game from her window, she calls J.J.'s dad, Artie (J.J.'s competetive, but nothing compared to his dad), at work at his law firm in Brooklyn. "This can't be happening," Brenda says. "Do something!" In the next scene, Artie is running out of his car and he blocks the ball at the last second. J.J. makes the winning shot, the Hills celebrate, and Kyle walks off a beaten man, all to the song "Time of Your Life."

When I was done editing it, I sat back in my computer chair and smiled. I was proud—pretty cool.

Frames taken from the actual video: J.J., about to lose; his dad saving the day. I wasn't sure how to use slow-motion, so I asked them to move slowly.

I hope they enjoy this.

Of course, my computer was giving me serious issues transferring the edited reel onto a DVD, so I barely made it to the dinner. Toward the end of the night, Coach K. put my tape in and they rolled down the dirty white screen for projection. Music started to play and everyone watched closely—well, I don't know if they did then, but whatever—it felt like that. There were oohs and aahs with some of the clips and the music, and I started to get nervous. Do they like it? As the video played, a few parents looked at me suspiciously. I had no idea why.

Then the video of J.J. and Kyle started playing. Suddenly, the audience erupted in cheers. My teammates and their family members jumped to their feet and went crazy. Our small forward, Ben, jumped up and down yelling "Amazing, amazing!"

I had never seen people respond like that to anything I'd done in my life. It made me think that maybe there was really something to this film stuff. Maybe I could actually do this.

The Star

SPOTLIGHT

Budding Spielberg eyes student film festival

By Matthew Jablonski

Weekend jaunts into Paris or the Swiss Alps were always boring for Andrew Jenks during his pre-adolescent years. Sitting in the back of his parent's car, a bulky pre-digital video camera helped him pass the time.

Today, the Hendrick Hudson High School junior still keeps his video equipment in tow wherever he goes.

Born in Rye, Jenks said his father's position with the United Nations necessitated multi-year stays for the family in Nepal and Belgium. His parent's weekend getaways to see the rest of Europe were supposed to be exciting. But Jenks used the time to hone his filmmaking abilities, conducting backseat interviews with his younger brother Matt and capturing on tape the people of Europe.

"Ever since I was four, I had
camera in my hands," Jenks sai
"Traveling around, there was nothin
else for me to do. That's how it
started."

Jenks is coordinating the Hendri
Hudson Film Festival — 25 studer
from Westchester and Putn
schools submitted original films t
will be judged in four categories
comedy, documentary, drama
experimental. Since Jenks will
judge in the May 17 competition
cannot submit any of his work.

In November, Jenks approac
principal Keith Schenker to ask
assistance in getting the idea of
ground. Schenker helped Jenk
cure a $1,000 school district gr
fund the festival.

"We have to find ways to ge
more involved in more constru
organized activities," Schenke
"I tell kids every year they s
present their new ideas to ad
tration."

Some students have good
but don't pursue them aggre
said Schenker, who complen
Jenks for being "goal-oriente

"He sets his mind to so
and he follows through," he
Last year, Jenks had a vari

Aaron Houston/The Star

Aspiring film-maker Andrew Jenks.

called "The Bench." The film spotlighted Chewning's trials and tribulations of being a substitute player on the team. Chewning said he had no problem being the subject for Jenks, who is the team's starting center.

"I didn't mind" Chewning said. "It was all fun and games. I love the sport of basketball, but I understand being 5' 5" with an okay jump shot is not starting material." Chewning said Jenks's talent won't remain anonymous for long.

"He's incredible," he said. "He's brilliant. I see him going places."

Jenks hopes to work as a production assistant this summer on a major television or movie set. Next year, he said, he'll try to get into Columbia University, where he'd like to study film. But when will he direct his first hit movie?

... 30," a confident
... household

Hendrick Hudson film buff organizing festival

by Adam Stone

If Andrew Jenks has his way, Hendrick Hudson High School is going Hollywood.

The 16-year-old junior is organizing a film festival for May 17, where students from Westchester and Putnam Counties can submit their work in four different genres – drama, comedy, documentary and experimental.

A seven-judge panel will present one award in each category.

On the big night, the auditorium will be jazzed up with old movie posters, and a rolling red carpet.

"I want there to be an Oscar feel," Jenks said.

With the help of a $1,000 grant from the district, Jenks is trying to court a keynote speaker for the event and is spreading the word about the festival. All submissions must be in by April 1.

The teenager wants to be a professional director one day, and is looking into Columbia and NYU film schools.

In fact, he's already working on creating his own documentary film company where he plans to chronicle the lives of a person or a family.

"I like the idea of taking a few words and ideas and transferring them onto film," Jenks said. "The best part is the satisfaction you get from the audience."

The young film buff, who is working on a short movie about family life, said he's found inspiration from a number of directors.

"I extol guys like Steven Spielberg, Steven Soderbergh, and of course Charlie Chaplin-the real renaissance man when it came to filmmaking, seemingly controlling all facets of film," Jenks said. "Then I can't forget Hitchcock who was so cool. Rather than putting actors on his movie posters, he put himself. I am going to bring that back."

Jenks is also part of a group called the Peers Influence Peers Partnership, where he's involved in the production of an anti-drug commercial.

The idea for a film festival has been stewing in Jenks' head since he was in eighth grade. And despite the pressure of SAT's and his A.P. classes, as well as a host of extracurricular activities the Cortlandt youngster participates in, the project is moving forward smoothly.

Principal Keith Schenker nodded his hat to Jenks for all his hard work.

"It's a niche that needs filling," Schenker said. "The credit goes to Andrew."

For more information on the film festival, call (914) or send an e-mail to HenHudFilmFest@aol.com.

ADAM STONE/North County News

Andrew Jenks poses with film equipment at Hen Hud High School.

Some local papers drum up support.

All-American High School Film Fest

At sixteen, I founded the Hendrick Hudson Film Festival for high school kids to show their films. When I needed a keynote speaker, a colleague of my mom's at a community health center who was good friends with James Earl Jones asked the star if he'd address a bunch of high school film geeks. I couldn't believe it when he agreed (I didn't tell him about my CNN fetish). He turned out to be one of the nicer people I have ever met. When I asked if he wanted to sit in the only air-conditioned room while the short films played (it was one

From left to right: Flyers for the festival, me and James Earl Jones on stage. I try and go back every year.

of the hottest days of the year, and my small public high school was baking), he asked if there was a seat for him with the rest of the audience. *What?* I thought. *He wants to sit in the heat and watch?* After I showed him to a seat, he thanked me for the honor of speaking at the film festival. A future Academy Award–winner thanking me for inviting him to this tiny festival? Talk about humble. He'll never know it but with his help, I'm proud to say, the festival is still going strong and has become one of the largest high school festivals in the world.

Wanting to make things with a camera was how I ended up at film school, where I got depressed. Everything around me was nonstop pretentious discussion about grandiose theories and technical camera angles, while I just wanted to tell a story as simple as J.J. beating Kyle. I thought the point of college was to form an opinion, but at NYU everyone seemed to already have one.

Jonah Quickmire Pettigrew was the only real friend I made at college. He was incredibly quiet and lived down the hall from me, but there was something about this Jonah guy. He was a bit pale, a bit small—definitely not the strongest guy I had ever seen (something we joked about a lot at college). And unlike nearly everyone else at college, he hardly came from money. Like me, all he knew was that he wanted to make movies—even if that meant going more than a hundred thousand dollars in debt. The son of a philosopher, Jonah had also made movies as a middle schooler, using snow-shoveling money to fund projects, like a movie about how hard it is to make a movie when you're thirteen years old. We got to know each other after I asked him to help me with my homework—aka give me his homework so I could copy from it—and because he's an incredibly nice guy, he did it. Without Jonah, I would never have passed freshman year. He'd get 100, and me, a suspicious 90 (I purposefully messed up here and there). Then I put up our homework side by side on my fridge like a proud parent.

Still, my social life was pretty bleak. If I wasn't watching *The West Wing* with my roommate or getting something to eat with Jonah at Mamoun's Falafel or Press Toast, I'd head over to the Comedy Cellar, a famous comedy club on MacDougal where it cost money to get in, so generally I just hung outside. But so did comics like Jim Norton and Louis C.K., who would smoke ciga-

Jonah getting ready for a music video we shot for Semi Precious Weapons, a band that now opens for Lady Gaga

rettes or talk shop in between sets. Occasionally I had the nerve to speak to them, like one time when I exchanged a few words with Judah Friedlander. But mostly I just eavesdropped on their conversations.

It was therapeutic to be around people who were actually doing something. Whether successful or not, these guys got up onstage. Me and all my fellow students just talked about doing something. I had been a good student in high school, the kind who joins any club that exists and wins awards like the humanitarian sportsman of the year, **but here, at college, I no longer had any real interests. I was lost.**

In August 1977, Grandad discovered a phosphor to be used in a lamp that gives 97% as much light as a standard lamp, but cuts the energy costs by 14%. This decreased the nation's electric bill by an estimated $770 million a year.

Me and Grandad around the same age

Grandad loved the simple things in life.

I wasn't the only one. In the winter of my freshman year, I took a trip with my mom to a nursing home to see my grandfather, an amazing man whom I had always looked up to, now suffering from dementia. Grandad was a genius, quite literally. He was a physicist with over 100 patents (I could barely pass chemistry).

But we were similar in a lot of little ways. First of all, people always said I looked like him when he was young.

We always played chess and tennis and had the same weird personality quirks. When he practiced tennis behind a local school, he liked to try to hit this small black dot on the wall over and over, exactly the kind of maniacal exercise I'd make up for myself.

Mom and me visiting Grandad during his last year. Even at his worst, he still loved drawing maps of galaxies. I didn't care if the maps were real or not, I loved him.

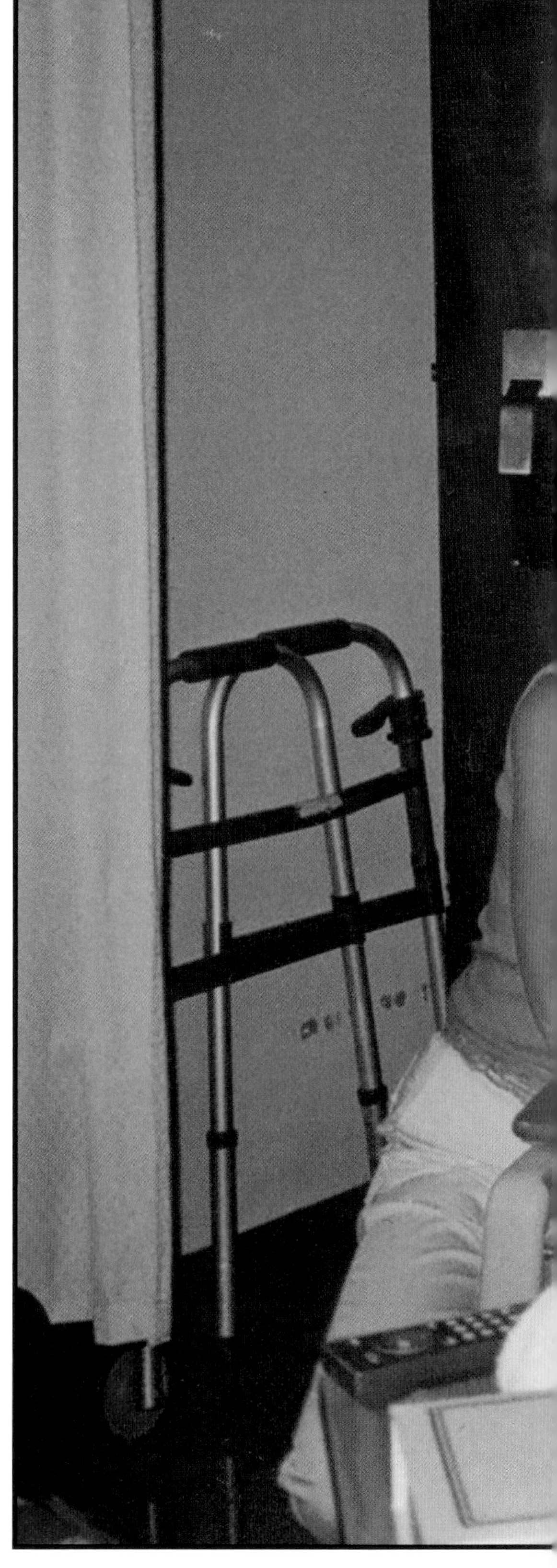

Now, in a facsimile of a living room with overstuffed couches and fake ficus plants, I hardly recognized Grandad. He sat in a chair looking past me, the sour smell of institutional food wafting in from the dining room.

"Hey, Grandad," I said.
"What's your name?" he asked.
"My name is Andrew."
"Oh, that'll be easy to remember, because my favorite grandson's name is Andrew."

I couldn't stand to see him like this, dying, in a way, and alone in a place that wasn't home. I started bawling, for my grandfather and, selfishly, for me. We were both isolated in these strange worlds, surrounded by strangers, and lacking in true freedom. The difference between my grandfather and me was that he had already had a whole life. I was just starting.

I'd had enough with college. I couldn't make films there, and, for me, the best way of learning was to go and do. I hated spending all my time sitting around watching and reading, so much so that I had stopped liking anything.

My only option was to blow this thing up.

chapter two

I WANT TO LIVE WITH OLD PEOPLE

COLLEGE
COLEGE
WHERE
RETIRE

Like all the best ideas, it was totally obvious. *Let's make a movie about a young guy who moves into a nursing home.*

I knew that the trailer I made in high school—from material I had shot during the summer before freshman year at a nursing home near my hometown and edited for most of the fall—was the perfect pitch tape to show to other assisted-living facilities I planned to approach about letting me move in. The tape, a "best of" from my senior citizen interviews with Beatles music playing underneath, was funny and sad all at the same time—exactly the kind of tone I was going for.

Musicians.
Inventors.
Teachers.
Salesmen.
A man who remembered the Great Depression like it was yesterday.
All kept prisoner in these homes.

I drafted a three-page outline to send to assisted-living facilities, articulating exactly how this thing was going to happen. I went online to find the perfect font for professional-looking letterhead.

"Upon completion, the feature documentary will be showcased at worldwide film festivals, such as Sundance and Cannes, and will then go on to be sold to cable channels like HBO and IFC," I wrote, and I kind of believed it.

With my best friend, Mom, during the winter in New York City when she came to see me because I was feeling particularly depressed.

Convincing myself of something has always been a major pastime of mine. I can be confident in my plans, bordering on arrogant. But deep down—way down—I am pretty fearful. I usually question whether I can really pull off my big idea. The internal debate about my actual abilities runs through the night. A lot of times, when I wake up in the morning, my teeth hurt from grinding.

With this idea, however, I felt more convinced, more confident than any other time in my life.

Unfortunately I was the only one. Everyone else thought I was crazy, or stupid, or usually both.

PROFESSOR 1

I don't know that you are the best person to do a study on what it's like to live in a nursing home.

PROFESSOR 2

You can't just go make a movie. That's hard. You have to get releases. Maybe they'd let you in for a couple of hours. *Maybe.* But I doubt it.

PROFESSOR 3

(blank, bored look)

Nobody is going to want to watch old people for ninety minutes. . . . See you next week in class.

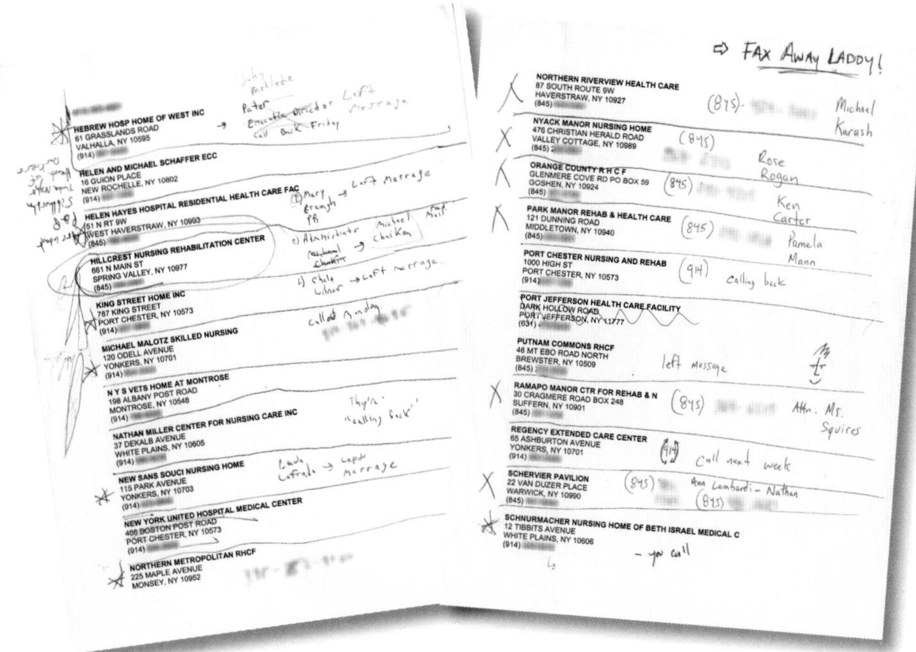

HEBREW HOSP HOME OF WEST INC
61 GRASSLANDS ROAD
VALHALLA, NY 10595
(914)

HELEN AND MICHAEL SCHAFFER ECC
16 GUION PLACE
NEW ROCHELLE, NY 10802
(914)

HELEN HAYES HOSPITAL RESIDENTIAL HEALTH CARE FAC
51 N RT 9W
WEST HAVERSTRAW, NY 10993
(845)

HILLCREST NURSING REHABILITATION CENTER
661 N MAIN ST
SPRING VALLEY, NY 10977
(845)

KING STREET HOME INC
787 KING STREET
PORT CHESTER, NY 10573
(914)

MICHAEL MALOTZ SKILLED NURSING
120 ODELL AVENUE
YONKERS, NY 10701
(914)

N Y S VETS HOME AT MONTROSE
198 ALBANY POST ROAD
MONTROSE, NY 10548
(914)

NATHAN MILLER CENTER FOR NURSING CARE INC
37 DEKALB AVENUE
WHITE PLAINS, NY 10605
(914)

NEW SANS SOUCI NURSING HOME
115 PARK AVENUE
YONKERS, NY 10703
(914)

NEW YORK UNITED HOSPITAL MEDICAL CENTER
406 BOSTON POST ROAD
PORT CHESTER, NY 10573
(914)

NORTHERN METROPOLITAN RHCF
225 MAPLE AVENUE
MONSEY, NY 10952

⇨ FAX AWAY LADDY!

NORTHERN RIVERVIEW HEALTH CARE
87 SOUTH ROUTE 9W
HAVERSTRAW, NY 10927
(845)
Michael Karash

NYACK MANOR NURSING HOME
476 CHRISTIAN HERALD ROAD
VALLEY COTTAGE, NY 10989
(845)
Rose Rogan

ORANGE COUNTY R H C F
GLENMERE COVE RD PO BOX 59
GOSHEN, NY 10924
(845)
Ken Carter

PARK MANOR REHAB & HEALTH CARE
121 DUNNING ROAD
MIDDLETOWN, NY 10940
(845)
Pamela Mann

PORT CHESTER NURSING AND REHAB
1000 HIGH ST
PORT CHESTER, NY 10573
(914)
calling back

PORT JEFFERSON HEALTH CARE FACILITY
DARK HOLLOW ROAD
PORT JEFFERSON, NY 11777
(631)

PUTNAM COMMONS RHCF
48 MT EBO ROAD NORTH
BREWSTER, NY 10509
(845)
left message

RAMAPO MANOR CTR FOR REHAB & N
30 CRAGMERE ROAD BOX 248
SUFFERN, NY 10901
(845)
Attn: Mrs. Squires

REGENCY EXTENDED CARE CENTER
65 ASHBURTON AVENUE
YONKERS, NY 10701
(914)
call next week

SCHERVIER PAVILION
22 VAN DUZER PLACE
WARWICK, NY 10990
(845)

SCHNURMACHER NURSING HOME OF BETH ISRAEL MEDICAL C
12 TIBBITS AVENUE
WHITE PLAINS, NY 10606
(914)

Two pages of my initial list of nursing homes to contact and try and move into. All of them were close to my home or at least in the New York Tri-state area. I eventually had to call outside of my area. I added the Mecca of senior living to my list . . . Florida.

Their dismissive attitude toward me served to charge me up. I was out to prove a point. But the professors weren't the only ones who didn't get it. The nursing homes didn't understand what I was talking about.

ME: I'd like to move into your home for a month or so.

ADMINISTRATOR: You sound young. How old are you?

ME: Nineteen. But you see . . .

ADMINISTRATOR: Oh no, this is a facility for senior citizens.

ME: I know; I want to see what it's like. . . .

ADMINISTRATOR: Young man, I think you are simply confused. What you're looking for is an apartment. There's a place down the street where all types of people live.

ME: I understand that. I want to move into your place.

ADMINISTRATOR (concerned): That doesn't make any sense. I'll get you the number for the place down the street. . . .

Calling dozens of nursing homes over the course of a day

After I told Jonah about my idea, he thought for a moment. "When are you leaving?" **I was a two-hundred-pound depressed nerd, but Jonah tried to convince me I was going to be the next Tom Cruise.**

"What the hell are you talking about?" I said, surprised that anyone would say something so absurd, but especially surprised that it was Jonah, who hardly said anything at all.

"You'll see," he said. "You're gonna have your own TV show and production company and make all kinds of movies. I know it."

I had pamphlets and video tapes of nursing homes from all over the country in my dorm room—more than any homework or tests. If the film thing didn't work out, I could be a consultant to anyone thinking of moving into an assisted living facility. Thirty phone calls later to nursing homes across the country . . .

KATHY CROLAND FROM HARBOR PLACE: Huh. A young person moving into a nursing home? That *is* an interesting idea. You could learn a lot here. Young people *should* do that. . . .

ME: I know, I know. It's a really good idea. And here's where it gets even better. The thing is, we don't just want to move in. It would be great to document this journey and make a film of some sort about the experience. So we would need full access to the place, obviously, to really get an idea of what it's like.

KATHY: Hmm . . . Yeah, filming the entire experience. Yeah, why wouldn't you? Don't just move in here! You should film what happens. Why hasn't someone ever done this before?

ME (lying): I know! I've had a lot of nursing homes say the same thing to me. As I said, we are in college, which means funds are kind of tight.

1 2 3
HANDLE ZOOM
AUDIO DUB
REC CHECK

The old camera I bought off of eBay

It'll be expensive enough for us to come down there, and we want to have a real experience, eating with the residents and everything, but we couldn't afford to pay for food.

KATHY: We always have extra food. Feeding you won't be a problem.

ME: Okay. Terrific. We also want to stay there—you know, to get the authentic experience—but again we can't afford to live where we live now let alone another place.

KATHY: Listen, my son is in college. I get what it is to be broke! He calls every day! We happen to have two vacant rooms; that shouldn't be a problem at all.

ME (cool on the outside, dying on the inside): I'll have to discuss it with my partners, but I think we may be able to make it work with you guys.

I had my location, the nursing home (Harbor Place). I had the cameraman (Jonah), and I got another NYU student, Will Godel, who had a van we could use to make the twenty-four-hour drive to Florida.

All I needed now was my star, a young guy who would be a funny and sympathetic tour guide through this land of old people.

I knew who I wanted immediately: Judah Friedlander.

This was before the comic became famous for his role on *30 Rock* and he was still just some dude outside the Comedy Cellar who wore weird trucker hats and old-man-style black-framed glasses. I liked him, I thought he was funny. I pitched him the idea outside the club one night, and he was down. We spoke on the phone a week later. “Sounds like a unique idea,” he said.

Budget for My Movie

Cameras purchased on eBay:	$1,206.00*
Audio equipment borrowed from a local high school:	$0.00
Gas to and from Florida:	234.00**
Two hundred and twenty MiniDV tapes:	358.60
Twelve Wendy’s meals on the road:	64.32
	$1862.92

*saved from my summer-camp job
**donation from Will’s dad

On the phone with the assisted living facility. Notice the fan.

"Call my manager so they can talk about the rate and all that crap." *The rate? And all that crap?* The thought of paying him hadn't even crossed my mind. I had no idea what his rate was, but it really didn't matter—there wasn't money for anyone to have a rate.

I went straight to a few of my friends. No way. I went down the list asking random people who might like free food and a trip to Florida. I couldn't get anyone to even think about it.

Finally I realized, no one is going to do this. I'm the only one who wants to do it. I should move in.

chapter three

SEX, OXYGEN TANKS, AND BINGO

335

Andrew Jenks

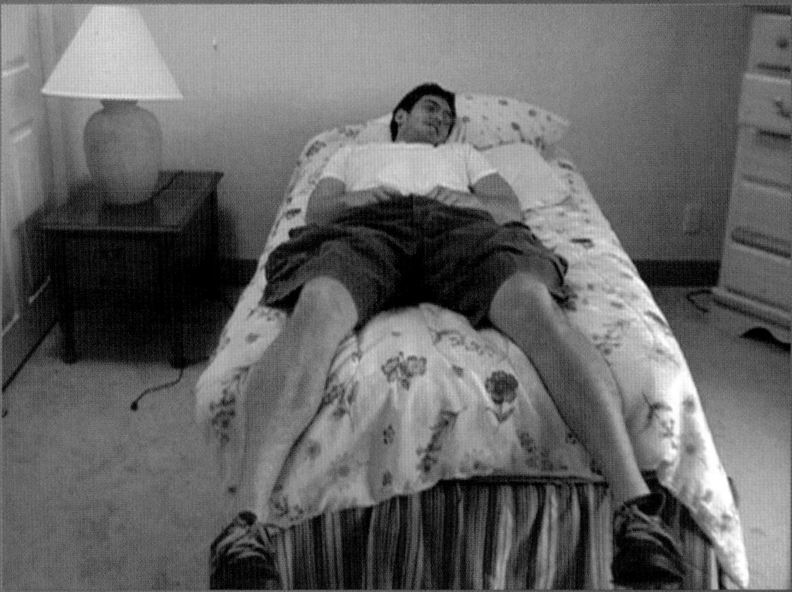

I lay in bed, staring up at the dark.

Man, I definitely made the worst decision of my life.

From the moment I arrived at Harbor Place, I felt stuck. The nursing home complex became a prison as soon as we were surrounded by these incredibly large walls. From the inside, there was no way to escape or see anything of the world.

On first walking into the main lobby, I introduced myself to the secretary, who was prepared for my arrival but not particularly interested in it. There was no special introduction. No hoopla for the new kid. She had work to do.

"Dinner is at four P.M. You already missed it," she said, handing me keys to Room 335.

For the first couple of weeks, the days were incredibly long.

I checked out the list of activities and joined whatever was going on—water aerobics, chair yoga—in an effort to meet people. Despite the board filled with events, by day two, I realized there was nothing really to do all day besides board games, TV watching, nail polishing, and mealtimes. And bingo.

Bingo was big.

At the daily six P.M. game, at least two dozen residents (all women) sat concentrating on their boards or making a crazy racket when somebody won. At least twice, a yelling match erupted, which resulted in a few residents getting the boot for the night (leaving some extra time to get ready for *Jeopardy!*). Although some people were resistant to being on camera, we filmed night and day. And we found some fascinating folks, but everything felt random and disjointed. We had lots of interviews but no cohesion, no story.

Two weeks in, we didn't have anything close to great footage and I was starting to panic. My mind had plenty of room to race in Harbor Place. At night, especially, it was eerily quiet. Hardly anyone else was awake past nine, when Jonah, Will, and I went down to the cafeteria to munch on cereal (you get hungry when you eat dinner at four P.M.). The place was totally deserted except for this guy George who did laps at night, passing us every ten minutes to stop and say, "Hey, fellas."

My bingo partner, Josie, who picked her cards using her childrens' birthdates, was the perennial champion.

JULY

Sunday	Monday	TUESDAY -	We
			7 10- 1:00-SIN 2:30-TIC 3:30- HUM CONTA 6-8-LOBE
			14 10- FANCY 1:00-SIN 2:30-FLIN 3:30-H CONTA 6-8-LOBB
18 10:30- TARGET TOSS -AR 1-2:15- PO-KE-NO-AR 2:30-3:30- SUNDAY COFFEE HOUR - AR	19 10-10:15-DAY'S ANNOUNCEMENTS-AR 10:30-PET THERAPY-AR 1-2:15-BOWLING -AR 2:30-RELAX TIME-AR 3:15- WDC VISITS-AR	20 10-10:15 - DAY'S ANNOUNCEMENTS-AR 10:30-BASKETBALL-AR 1:00-FLING-A-RING-AR 2:30-WORD GAME-AR 6-8-LOBBYLOUNGERS L.	21 10-FANC 1:00-SIN 2:30-TIC-T 3:30-H CONTAGE 6-8-LOBE
25 10:30-TARGET TOSS 1-1:30-INTERFAITH CHURCH SERVICES-AR 1:30- WORD GAME -AR 2:30-3:30- SUNDAY COFFEE HOUR -AR	26 10:-10:15-DAY'S ANNOUNCEMENTS-AR 10:30-PET THERAPY-AR 1-2:15-BOWLING -AR 2:30-RELAX TIME-AR 3:15-WDC VISITS-AR	27 10-10:15- DAY'S ANNOUNCEMENTS-AR 10:30-BASKETBALL-AR 1:00-CURRENT EVENTS 2:30-JULY BIRTHDAY PARTY -AR 6-8-LOBBYLOUNGERS	28 10-FANC 1:00-SIN 2;30-FLIN 3:30-HUM CONTA 6-8-LOBB

Evening Bingo
6-7pm

BARBEQUE

Lobby Loungers Tuesday

EVENT CALENDAR

sday	Thursday	Friday	Saturday
	1 10-10:15 DAY'S ANNOUNCEMENTS-AR 10:30-SITTERCISES-AR 1:00-TABLE GAMES-AR 2:30-FRUIT SALAD-AR 3:30- TRIVIA -AR 6-LOBBY LOUNGERS-L		
CY FINGER -LONG-AR C-TOE-AR IS OUS -AR OUNGERS L.	8 10-10:15- DAY'S ANNOUNCEMENTS-AR 10:30-SITTERCISES-AR 1:30-FOOTINGS GROUP -AR 2:30-FRUIT SALAD-AR 3:30-4-TRIVIA -AR		
5- GERS-AR -LONG-AR -RING-AR OR IS OUS -AR UNGERS	15 10-10:15-DAY'S ANNOUNCEMENTS-AR 10:30-SITTERCISES-AR 1:00-2:15-TAI-CHI-AR 2:30-FRUIT SALAD-AR 3:30-4- TRIVIA -AR 6-8-LOBBY LOUNGERS	16 10-10:15-DAY'S ANNOUNCEMENTS-AR 10:15- MUSIC BY AL-AR 1-2:15- MOVIE -AR 2:30-SHORT STORY-AR 6-8-LOBBY LOUNGERS	17 10-11:15-Shuffle Board AR 1-3 -SATURDAY MOVIE MATINEE AR 3-3:30- MOVIE DISCUSSION-AR
NGERS-AR -LONG-AR TOE-AR OR IS S -AR OUNGERS			24 10-11-SHUFFLEBOARD A.R 1-3-SATURDAY MOVIE MATINEE-AR 3-3:30-MOVIE DISCUSSION-AR
NGERS-AR -LONG-AR -RING-AR S OUS -AR UNGERS			31 10-11:15-Shuffle Board AR 1-3-SATURDAY MOVIE MATINEE-AR 3-3:30-MOVIE DISCUSSION-AR

AR-Activity Room O-Outdoors
L - Lobby
C - Chapel

Sometimes, when George passed, I would think about what he was like when he was young, before he'd lost his mind. What was he like in high school? Did he have a wife and kids? What had he done for work? It was depressing to think I was probably the only one who even thought about it; this guy was alone. His dementia made communication hard, so only once could I really understand him. "What do I think of this place?" he asked, answering the question himself. "I want to get the hell out."

On the way to the dollar store with Bill. He referred to these daily walks outside the walls as his "great escape."

By eleven P.M., there was nothing left to eat or say. I returned to Room 335, which was small and clean, with white walls, a tiny bed, a rocking chair, and a giant handicapped bathroom. There was nothing wrong with it, but I hated spending time in there. The question of what the hell I was doing kept me up at night. Every minute that passed, the predictions of THOSE professors became more valid.

Surrounded by darkness and quiet, I thought, *We better get something soon, or this is going to be a disaster.*

DAY 2
DAY 3
DAY 4
DAY 5
DAY 6
DAY 8
DAY 9
DAY 10
DAY 11
DAY 12
DAY 13
DAY 15
DAY 16
DAY 18
DAY 19
DAY 20
DAY 22
DAY 23

Tammy said in the hospital, "Ya know, we're put on this Earth to try and make people happy. And it doesn't take much to make somebody feel good." This is the first time I met her, and she already had us laughing.

"You the college boy moving in?" said a lady with big glasses.

"Uh-huh."

"Oh, for goodness' sake, you're in for some trouble, baby."

"Oh yeah?"

"You just don't know," she said, holding up a plastic bag in one arthritic hand. "I just got my medicine."

"What's that?"

"My birth control pills."

Here we go.

That was Tammy, a tiny 96-year-old who didn't let the fact that she could hardly see, hear, or walk get in the way of a good time. Her hilariousness brought a glimmer of hope to everyone and I was no exception. With her, I had the feeling that my movie had a chance of not being the biggest flop ever.

I was just starting to pick up the energy of a story happening when I got called into Kathy Croland's office, which was like getting called into the principal's office. We had screwed up, clearly, but I had no idea how. Nothing stood out. Maybe we were filming too much, or eating too much. I wasn't sure. Kathy closed the door to her office behind me.

"Andrew," she began.

She's going to kick me out. This whole thing is back to a failure.

"You said you wanted to be a resident here and be a part of this experience."

I do. I do!

"I let you stay in our rooms and eat our food."

Oh God.

"A big rule that we have at Harbor Place is that you have to wear pants to the dining room during dinnertime. People are telling me that you are wearing shorts. You can't do that."

That's it?

"All right," I said. "You got it. I promise it won't happen again. Pants. Definitely."

That night, I kept my word and wore pants to dinner. A guy in a Hawaiian shirt, wearing glasses with thick black plastic frames (not unlike Judah Friedlander's) came up to me. After giving me the once-over, he said,

"Wearing pants, huh?"

"Yep."

"Someone told you that was a rule?" he said, looking down at his own legs. He was wearing shorts. "Sucker," he said.

That was Bill.

Bill loved to "hang out." He was always, as he said, "walking around and walking around." It's how we got to know him so well.

Tammy and Bill were opposite sides of the same turning point. They connected me to something deeper than the quirks of the elderly at permanent camp, to something about the human spirit and not giving up.

One night, I heard banging on the door.

"What the . . ."

Loud banging.

I jumped. It must have been midnight.

I opened the door to find Jonah and Will sweating—
Jonah, with camera in hand as always, trying to catch his breath.

"Dude, it's chaos. The electricity went out. People don't know . . . Just come!"

It was mostly pitch-dark except for backup lights in the hallway. I put some clothes on and started walking around with the guys. Most of the residents were fast asleep. But certainly not all of them. We looked around for staff, but at this hour, there were only a few employees on the premises. And there were a few hundred residents. We heard people talking from their rooms, even yelling, and realized we had to split up.

Jonah followed an elderly woman with dementia around the hallway. "I got up because I couldn't see, and now I forget where my room is," she explained.

They walked around for a while until she finally found it. I remember watching the footage a month or so later and thinking Jonah played it perfectly. He never stopped filming, but also comforted the woman as he helped her locate her room. When they arrived, he realized the reason she had gotten up in the first place: She had peed in her bed.

FULL
2000
1000
0

Primitive Storytelling

This is a concept I came up with early on to help me understand the process of making a documentary. Later, I realized things are more complicated.

1. When you start on one of these things, it is you and the subject side by side but separate.

2. Then you start to get to know the subject and become closer to his or her story.

3. If you're doing a good job, the subject starts to feel closer to you. You kind of become friends.

4. At a certain point, you go deeper, push harder, and the subject backs away.

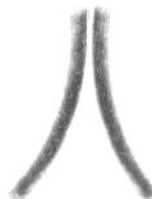

5. Finally, the subject returns on a full level of trust.

6. When it's over, there is only one takeaway, whether it's good, bad, or inconclusive.

Nobody loves going to an old age home, not even old people. And few love visiting them either, which isn't lost on its residents. Many, like Tammy, had outlived all their friends and family, so there was simply no one to visit them. But others with relatives didn't get too many visits either, and when they did get one, it served less as a diversion and more as a reinforcement of their predicament. Mildred, an aggressively successful bingo player, brought this to my attention.

"You saw how my daughter came to visit?" Mildred asked me.
"Yeah, that was really nice," I answered.
"Did you see how many times she looked at her watch?"

I realized in so many moments like that one with Mildred that the people living there were a lot more in tune than we give them credit for.

If you visit for forty-five minutes but look at your watch ten times, it's like you weren't really there at all.

I thought I was going in to make a movie about a nursing home, but on the long drive home, I realized I was making a movie about a group of friends. I thought I was going to make a movie about old people, but left knowing that the movie was about Tammy, Bill, Libby, Dotty, Josie, Eleanor . . .

I couldn't wait to leave. But at the same time, it was so hard to leave.

It was very depressing, and at first that's all it was. But as I got closer to a few of the residents and started to see the world through their eyes, I realized something pretty amazing. The residents of Harbor Place didn't have much left in the way of energy or abilities, but whatever they had left they used to give back to someone else.

Like with Tammy. She could hardly walk or see or hear, but her mind was totally there. So during dining hours, she'd have her pal Libby roll her from gloomy table to gloomy table to gloomy table, and by the time she was rolling away, she'd have that table laughing, if only for a minute . . . if only for a moment.

Bill, meanwhile, had terrible dementia. Most of the time he couldn't remember my name not long after we'd just had a conversation. But what he could do, unlike most people there, was walk. He was actually really strong. When he'd pull my arm, it would hurt. He snuck out every single day to the dollar store, where he'd buy four or five different kinds of candies. He had diabetes, which prevented him from eating candy. But the treats weren't for him. When he returned to Harbor Place, he'd give them out. He couldn't remember names, but he never forgot his route or the candy preferences of the residents and staff members.

Witnessing the daily actions of Bill, Tammy, and the rest gave me confidence in being alive that I definitely didn't have before.

They had every reason to be angry. To feel abandoned. But they used whatever energy they had to help one another. Maybe Tammy couldn't walk or hear properly, but she could tell a classic sex joke. And if that made you

smile, she'd done her job. Maybe Bill couldn't remember what he talked about earlier in the day, but he could walk and get candy for you. Once he handed that piece of candy off and saw the happy face, he was proud. He would nod, start whistling, and walk back toward his room. I had never seen, firsthand, the natural instinct to give even when you have lost everything.

chapter four
THE BIG TIME (SORT OF)

After I moved out of Room 335, I moved into my parents' basement for the rest of the summer, where I edited the movie down from two hundred hours of footage that I kept track of with a semidetailed calendar. Watching and rewatching that period in time was like having the experience all over again, except on steroids. I lived the lessons I learned at Harbor Place again and again with each new expression, comment, or gesture I had missed in the moment.

My high school friends (and even friends of friends) would come over at all hours of the day. Some before work, some after. Some late-night after a party. A few watched scenes before going to sleep. Regardless of who it was, I liked to see how people reacted to the material. Were they watching? Laughing? Tearing up? A few times a day, I would whip together a couple of recently edited pieces to get my friends' thoughts.

They would hate it or love it, and regardless, I would get back to work.

A very late night in my dirty basement, trying to find a particular moment in my log calendar...

June 2005

Nagoya JAPAN

Did you know... Japan is baseball-mad, and Nagoya is no exception. In 1997 the city built a state-of-the-art 40,500-seat domed stadium for its hometown heroes, the Chunichi Dragons.

WEEK 25 22

20 MONDAY ~~22A~~

22A: Betty + Karl eating lunch w/George

8 (lunch sequence)

• ~~Bill eating~~ lunch sequence

9 • HP in rain (few)

• Phillis off van

10 • Andrew + Libby "where's Tommy"

• Bill w/ us w/ camera

11 22B: • Lunch sequences

• HP in rain

Lunch • Andrew w/ Libby

22C: • talking: Andrew + Joe Carter

12 • Hallway fading

• Arts + crafts

1 • Will + Jonah looking w/ camera

• Tea party w/George

2 • Tea party w/ Karl, friends, Andrew

• Sophie to room

3 22D:

• Andrew + Libby waiting for Tommy

4 ↳ Tommy arrives

• Libby Disappear

5 • checking mailboxes show shot arts + crafts

• Me + Maggie + George

6 • Karl + Betty down Hallway

• Maggie convo / Maggie fade

7 • other Will + Jonah shot

• ~~with~~ Angry woman at Bingo

22E: Andrew + Josephine Bingo (fight night)

• Disappearing shot of Bingo

21 TUESDAY 23A

22F/23A:

• Bingo (woman fighting)

8 • hi to Mary at Elevator

• exotic birds

9 23B: exotic birds

• Celina sleeping

10 • Karl + Betty, George + GF looking for Kathie

11 • sleeping Celina

• convo w/ Josie

Lunch 23C:/24A

• convo w/ Josie

12 23D:

• Ann Greenspan

1 • Jaceline

• Angry Bill

2 • Purple Mary

23E:/24B

3 • Purple Mary

Summer begins (summer solstice)

22 WEDNESDAY 24

23C/24A: Josie talk

• Bus footage • Beach footage

8 24B: • Bus footage

• Beach footage / Lunch

9 24C: • Beach / Lunch

"the All" • Bus footage

10 ↳ Bill + Andrew singing

23F 24D: Bus footage

11 ↳ Bill + Andrew singing

• woman sleeping • old young old man

Lunch • Ballet • Libby in elevator

• Libby w/ crackers, Walter + Tommy + Libby Fa

12 • Marge convo

24E • Tippy interview

1 24F: Marge

• Karl + Betty convo outside

2 • Hallway w/ Mary Jordan

• Tommy + Jeopardy

3 24G: Beach "the Fall"

• Beginning of Tippy interview

4 • Ruth + Mary interview Jeopardy

24H

5 w/ Tommy

6

7

Every night we tried to log each tape in some American Express calendar I'd found.

My parents' small, concrete, smelly, oftentimes flooded basement (at night we had to put everything on tables just in case)

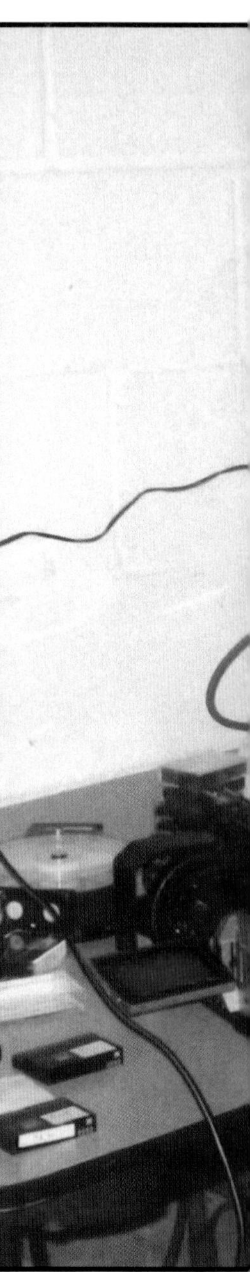

The tremendously hard worker and good friend Will Godel, falling asleep in the basement

When I felt like I had a solid ninety-minute movie, I started submitting it to random film festivals that I found online. "Is this Andrew Jenks?" asked a big-time film festival director over the phone. "I received your film *Room 335*."

My heart started to pump with that scared, happy kind of adrenaline, the kind you get when you leap from some high jumping spot into water, kiss a new girl you really like, or get a call from a film festival after receiving written rejections from dozens of others.

"We're in!"
"Oh no."
"Huh?"
"I'm calling to tell you that we can't accept your film."
"Oh."
"And, really, I think you should stop sending this film out. It's not going to get into *any* festivals. You're wasting everyone's time is all, including your own."

What? That was like applying to college and not only getting rejected but having the dean of admissions call you up to tell you *not* to go to college. Anywhere. Despite the severity of this rejection (which made the other form letters seem like love notes), I didn't think of giving up. Sure, I questioned what I was doing, but by this point I had a ninety-minute movie that I really believed in. There was no turning back now. I had already heard "no" plenty of times since I started this project. So, Mr. Film Festival Director, thanks for the advice, but I am going to leave it at the table.

Jan 28, 2006

Dear Filmmaker,

Thank you for your entry to The Garden State Film Festival. We appreciate you
sharing your fine work with us. We regret to inform you that due to an overwhelming
amount of excellent entries, we will not be able to show your film this year at our
festival. Please take heart knowing that many really wonderful films will not be
screened due to the small amount of screening time we have available. We hope you
will plan to join us on March 31 - April 2nd at the historic Paramount Theater- built
in 1910, on the boardwalk in Asbury Park, NJ for this marvelous opportunity to meet
other independent and veteran filmmakers.

Pouring through old emails I was surprised to find so many rejection letters from very random film festivals.

Thank you for submitting your film to the 2006 Sedona International
Film Festival. Regretfully, I must inform you that it was not selected by
our committee. We appreciate having had the opportunity to view your
work, and want you to know that the decision was a difficult one, as we
saw many more worthy films than we had space for.

I would like to wish you the best of luck with this project and your
forthcoming work. I hope that you will give the festival the same
consideration in the future.

So many people said no that the word became a turn-on. It became my starting point.

Dear Andrew:

Thank you for the opportunity to preview ANDREW JENKS, ROOM 335. We
appreciated seeing your work, but I am sorry to tell you that it has not been
selected for the 12th Annual Los Angeles Film Festival.

The modest size of our Festival means that many wonderful and deserving
productions will not be included in this year's Festival. We wish you
success with the film and hope you will keep us informed about your future
projects.

Thanks again for your interest in the Los Angeles Film Festival.

May 11, 2006

Hello,

Thank you very much for submitting to the CineVegas Film Festival.
Unfortunately we did not select your film this year. As the festival screens
a low number of films — around 30 features and 25 short films — it makes it
hard to show as many good film as are out there.

We wish you the best of luck with the film and hope to see your future work

Sincerely,

Thank you for sending in your film in order to be considered for selection into the 35th
International Film Festival Rotterdam.

We have made our final selections for our 2006 programme, and to our regret we have
to inform you that your film ANDREW JENKS, ROOM 335 has not been included.

Because of the enormous amount of submitted films, it's impossible for us to give you
further details of our decision. We do hope for your understanding.

Still we like to thank you for the (ongoing) interest shown in our festival and we do hope
that you will not hesitate to contact us with new projects in the future.

I'm glad I didn't listen to that guy and burn all my copies of the movie, because finally, thankfully, ecstatically, we got into a festival, and it was an awesome one: the Santa Barbara International Film Festival.

Jonah and I were so excited, we got to the Southern California city a week early to drum up an audience for our film. Our lodging at a scary motel thirty miles outside the city didn't do anything to dispel the idea that we were big-timing it.

Walking up to the second floor of the movie theater the night of our screening, my throat was dry and my palms were sweaty. It was about forty-five minutes before the film premiered, but when I got to the top, there was a giant line. For another movie. Ben Affleck had one premiering at the same exact time.

Bottom Left: Outside the motel
Top Right: Inside small motel I shared with Jonah, pizza box on bed that we relied on for quite a few days
Bottom Left: Straight from the airport to do a local morning show
Bottom Right: At Cinequest Film Festival, where two of my friends came, only to find out I required them to wear "Bill Hawaiian shirts" to promote the film.

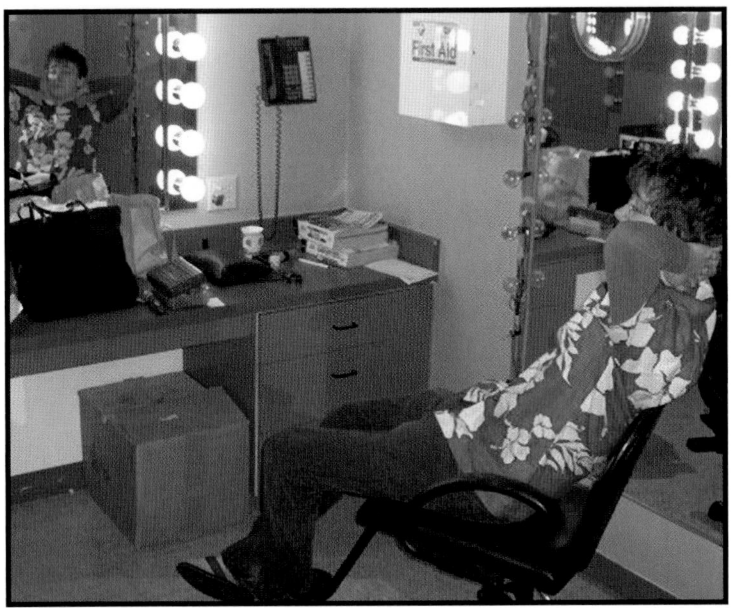
First Aid

www.
AndrewJenks
Room335
.com

Welcome
to the
Santa Barbara International Film Festiva
Film

SPONSORS
SCREAM

What did I ever do to you, Ben Affleck? I thought to myself. I always loved *Good Will Hunting*.

As I got closer to the line that I was sure was for the Oscar winner's movie, someone approached me. "Hey, you're the guy in the old-person movie, right?" he said. "Not a bad line this early before showtime."

When the lights went down inside the packed movie theater, with my parents and Jonah by my side, I felt like Steven Spielberg.

Then the movie started.

Apparently I was not an expert at sound design. I had put in the right music and lips were in sync with dialogue. Final Cut, the program I'd used to edit the movie, unbeknownst to me had leveled out the sound. When I transferred the movie to a Beta tape, it went back to being out of whack. Big lesson. Tammy's words came out like a whisper. Then, out of nowhere, *Jeopardy!* playing on a TV set in the background blasted everyone in the theater out of their seats. Someone in the audience shouted, "Oh!" This was bad.

Top Left: The night I arrived in Santa Barbara, shocked there was a car picking us up. Even excited they had a banner. Jonah and I had spent the flight over letting passengers know about our screening times.
Top Right: Jonah before the premiere, terrified
Bottom Left: Opening night of the film festival
Bottom Right: With my best friend, Dan Zinn, at Cinequest Film Festival

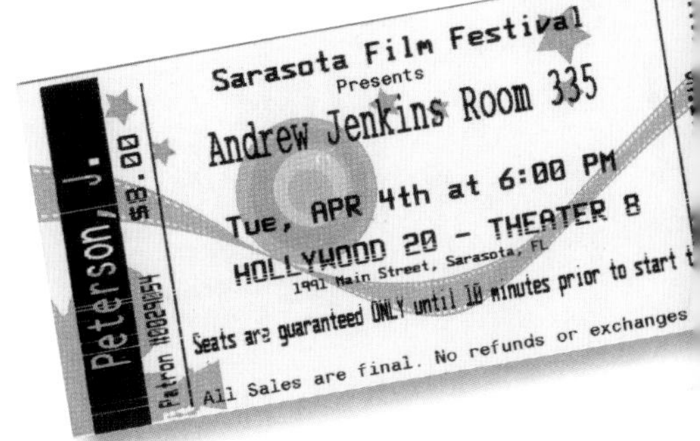

The postcards we went EVERYWHERE with

My name is Andrew Jenks and I am 19 years old. I always thought I could learn a lot from old people. And so this summer I moved into an assisted living facility in Florida. My life will never be the same.

Andrew Jenks
Room 335

Santa Barbara International Film Festival
World Premiere **February 4, 2006 4pm**
Second Screening **February 7, 2006 9pm**
Theater **Center Stage Theater**
www.andrewjenksroom335.com

He wanted to live with old people.
But was he ready for this?

Andrew Jenks
Room 335

"Riveting!"
James Ronald Whitney,
Emmy-award winner, Best Documentary

Despite the sound problems, when the movie ended, the place cheered loudly. (A few audience members kindly and gently let us know that the movie was very hard to watch this way—and it didn't get any easier during the screenings throughout the week. Because I couldn't fix the sound, every showing was like a punch in the face. I had to brace myself and watch the audience in discomfort.)

We stumbled out of the screening, shell-shocked, and the festival employee who had been taking tickets stopped to tell me that "Henry Winkler came, but he couldn't get in because there wasn't a seat."

What?

"You didn't let the Fonz in? I have seen this a million times. I didn't need to see it again. You could have given him my seat. How did you not let the Fonz in?"

Jonah and I during our first Q and A... something that we ended up doing all over the world. I thought this was going to be my first and last time talking about the movie.

Reed Business Information.

VARIETY

100 YEARS

VARIETY.COM ▪ THE INTERNATIONAL ENTERTAINMENT WEEKLY ▪ FEB. 27 - MARCH 5, 2006

Andrew Jenks, second from left, with friends Tammy Signorile, left, Bill Delarm, and Libby Smith in docu "Andrew Jenks Room 335."

ANDREW JENKS ROOM 335

(DOCU)

A Hemi Prods. presentation. Produced, directed by Andrew Jenks. Camera (color, DV), Jonah Quickmire Pettigrew; editors, Jenks, Pettigrew; music, Tom Obedlam; music supervisor, Sean O'Neill; sound, Jenks, Pettigrew; assistant director, William Godel. **Reviewed at Santa Barbara Film Festival,** Feb. 4, 2006. **(Also in Cinequest Film Festival.)** Running time: **89 MIN.**

With: Andrew Jenks, Bill Delarm, Tammy Signorile, Libby Smith, Dotty Shepard, Dr. Steve Cowan.

By ROBERT KOEHLER

Part sociological experiment, part docu diary, "Andrew Jenks Room 335" combines the chutzpah of the tyro, titular 19-year-old filmmaker deciding to live among elderly in various states of health, and a fine sensitivity to its subject. What could have been solipsistic is a lovely and genuine account of generational understanding, and a wonderful display of the inherent advantages of the tiny 24p vid camera. Fests should compete heavily for this unorthodox look at aging, while micro distribs can consider it an ideal counter-programmer.

Spending little time noodling over why he even wants to do this, Jenks tells his skeptical therapist, Dr. Steve Cowan, that he would like to spend 36 days in a Florida assisted care facility. "They're outcasts," says Jenks in one of his few self-revealing statements. "Sounds right for me."

With lenser Quickmire Pettigrew and a.d. William Godel by his side, Jenks settles at the Harbor Place facility in Port St. Lucie, Fla., and makes friends with a wide range of residents.

At 95, Tammy Signorile is one of the liveliest of Jenks' neighbors, a spirited companion for nearly-blind Libby Smith and Dotty Shepard, who grows gravely ill over June 2005 period of filming.

Eighty-year-old Bill Delarm initially strikes Jenks as aloof and uncommunicative, but it's a measure of Jenks' friendly nature and filmmaking determination that he gets him to open up. As they mock-spar and roughhouse with each other, Jenks evidently also needs Delarm, one of the facility's few men, as a kind of macho playmate.

Jenks and his crew keep the tradition of verite cinema going by simply capturing what happens in front of the camera, including a fairly terrifying sequence when the Harbor Place's power goes out during a tropical storm, leaving a few dementia patients alone in the dark. Visibly shaken by the 36 days, Jenks sadly departs on July 4, torn between hating to say goodbye to his new friends and clearly stressed by the dead, dying and persons with infirmities that have surrounded him.

Given the circumstances, pic is raw but eminently viewable, while sound is smudged at several points. Though never intrusive, Tom Obedlam's score inserts a jangly, even slightly disturbing edge.

Variety, a top trade magazine in the film industry

Jonah and I tried to make up for the Fonz debacle by personally handing out *Room 335* DVDs to a bunch of celebrities at the festival.

They were all really nice. I have no idea if any of them watched it.

I found out three weeks later that a review ran in *Variety* only because agents started calling my number. Mark Burnett's (TV producer) agent was among them.

"I represent the best of the best," he said. "You give Mark and my team ninety days, we'll make real money. Not this documentary crap."

As I walked down Washington Square West to get cheap pizza at Ben's, I was partly intimidated. But somehow the aggressive agent couldn't dissuade me from pursuing my goal to show *Room 335* on HBO, the premiere channel for documentary films—which I let him know.

I am hoping one day I'll be wise enough to honestly say I don't read my own reviews.

Photos by Jonah Quckmire Pettigrew

Top, Andrew Jenks counts the days he spent in the nursing home.
Above, Tammy, Andrew Jenks, Bill and Libby, residents of the Florida nursing home.

From college dorm to nursing home, at 1

After his grandpa's struggles, filmmaker gets up c

...ths later,

TALK TO THE HAND

The good old boy

An NYU student gives assisted living a whirl in *Andrew Jenks, Room 335.*

By **Bilge Ebiri**

The idea of a college student checking himself into a senior facility sounds like either a desperate cry for help or the premise for a tasteless comedy. But Andrew Jenks, it's soon apparent, is no ordinary college student. In 2005, as a freshman at NYU, Jenks looked around at th... other 19-year-olds he... and wondered what i... to live with 300 elderl... the time, my grandfat... been an inventor for G... had been really close to... infection and then deme... course of three weeks, to... where he could no longer remember my name," he recalls. "And I was at college, where all you do is think about the future. I wondered what it's like on the flip side of this: Are you still thinking about the future? Are you thinking about the past? It seemed like a strange position to be in in life."

So Jenks checked himself into the Harbor Place senior residence in Florida for the summer. Two of his college friends, Jonah... Pettig...

Jenks didn't set any hard-and-fast rules for himself and his crew, except that they would not do anything the seniors weren't doing (aside, obviously, from filming). "In other words, we couldn't just get up and drive to the mall if we wanted to. We lived there and did the things they were doing." Soon the three young filmmakers became very clo... number of th...

making wasn't a movie about old people, but a movie about Tammy and Bill and Dotty and Libby."

While focusing on specific residents, Jenks admirably avoids a clinical approach to his subject matter, generally not addressing specific health problems. "We knew them as people," he says. "And you don't sit there thinking about this person having Alzheimer's or that person having dementia." At the same time, the filmmakers felt it was important to show the bad as well as the good: "If we were showing the happy moments—Tammy telling jokes and Bill walking to the store to get candy for the other residents—it

> "We couldn't just get up and drive to the mall if we wanted to."

wouldn't have been fair for us not to show the rougher patches," Jenks says. As a result, the film's most devastating instance comes when Shepard's health fails for good; Jenks sits by her quivering body in the hospital, speaking to her and praying with her. "When we were editing the film, we really thought long and hard about whether to include these scenes," the filmmaker recalls.

Although a number of the residents featured in the film have since died, Jenks has kept in touch with the folks at Harbor Place, and got a chance to show the film to his subjects before they passed away. In the meantime, though, he has had to split his time with other projects: Last March, he traveled to Japan to film his next documentary, financed by ESPN, about former Dodgers player and Mets manager Bobby Valentine's attempts to restore the popularity of baseball in that country as manager of the Chiba Lotte Marines. Not bad for someone who is still, technical... Jenks...

TIMEOUTNEWYORK.COM

Tuesday, January 15, 2008

Weather: Light snow possible, 41/30 SPORTS ★ FINAL

DAILY NEWS

34 **THE DAILY GRIND** A Q&A WITH A WORKING NEW YORKER

A youthful filmmaker in residence

EIGHT QUESTIONS FOR ...

a documentary maker

Your first documentary, "Andrew Jenks, Room 335," debuts tonight on [redacted]. What inspired you to check into a Florida assisted-living facility in 2005 to film the lives of senior citizens?

I was living in a dorm freshman year [at NYU] with 300 other 19-year-olds. Meanwhile, I was really close to my grandfather. He got an infection in his foot, and from there just slowly deteriorated and ended up in a nursing home. It was really sad to see someone who was so on top of things and so bright get to that stage. These two things intersecting left me asking myself what would it be like to be that old.

Why did you choose Harbor Place in Port St. Lucie?

People thought the camera would cause a lot of facilities to say no. With most of the places that we called, it wasn't the cameras that were a problem; it was my age. The first thing we would ask is, "Would you let a 19-year-old live there?" Most said absolutely not, you have to be 65, so that was usually the end of the conversation. Harbor Place was really nice to us. It's a great facility, and they do everything they can for their residents.

What were your expectations going into this project?

I was thinking it would be a movie about them going to bingo and waking up and having breakfast at 6 a.m. In the end, the movie was about my friends: Tammy, Bill, Libby ... these characters that I met. You couldn't write better lines than what Tammy says.

Did you experience any culture shock in hanging out with 94-year-olds?

I was called into the general manager's office, and the manager comes in and says, "There's been some complaints." I'm like, oh my God, who did we offend? Did we film something we weren't supposed to? And she says, "You know it's a rule in the dining hall that when you eat dinner, you need to wear pants. I've had at least five residents come to me and say that you're wearing shorts to dinner. If you are going to be a resident at Harbor Place, you need to wear pants." From then on, I wore pants!

Andrew Jenks

AGE: 21

JOB: Documentary filmmaker

HOURS/WEEK: During a project, he's filming, on call or editing 24/7

TIME ON THE JOB: Two years

SALARY: "I do well, but I'm not contractually allowed to speak about this."

any of this would happen. We hoped that maybe our parents would watch it, maybe it would show at a film festival. In terms of [redacted parent company] HBO calling us, I don't think that was ever in our mind-set.

What has changed?

I have an editing space now [living in the Financial District] instead of working in my parents' basement.

I'm not a typical film-school kid. [At NYU] I was studying general film courses, but I don't watch a lot of movies. I just really enjoy going out there and making them more than anything.

For your next project, how do you top shacking up in an assisted-living home?

I actually just got back from Japan. We were there for eight months working on a documentary [for ESPN] about Bobby Valentine, who managed the New York Mets and took them to the World Series. Then he went to Japan, where the game is dying. He's literally saving the game. It's about this 55-year-old man whose ...

Jenks hanging out with some of his fellow residents at Harbor Place, a retirement and assisted-living complex in Port St. Lucie, Fla.

turned drinking age.

It's hard to think of anything else besides what we're working on ... even if we're living in New York City. I think my generation is cast as a ...

seriously, and I don't think that's ac... This generation can do a lot to chang... You'll see a lot more of us. Nico...

"Andrew Jenks, Room 335" premi... at 7 exclusively

NEW YORK POST

25¢ CENTS

TUESDAY, JANUARY 15, 2008 / Mainly cloudy with a flurry, 40 / Weather: Page 42 ★★

LATE CITY FINAL

www.nypost.com

Old folks at home

LINDA STASI
TV Critic

"Andrew Jenks, Room 335"

★★★★

Andrew Jenks (second from left) moves in the with the forgotten demographic in "Room 335" tonight.

College kid's real senior year

SOME 19-year-olds spend their summers trying to find where the latest "Girls Gone Wild" is being filmed.

Some get jobs.

And only one that we know of decided to move into an assisted-living facility and make a film of his own.

It could have been called, "Old Folks Gone Wise," but this 19-year-old, Andrew Jenks, decided to call his film simply "**Andrew Jenks, Room 335.**"

It's so good that it doesn't need a fancy name.

The show Jenks made is the story of his 30-odd days living in an old-folks home in Florida called Harbor Place. Not a sad, horrid story of abuse or even one of simply watching the machine break down, this is the story of a kid who figured that old people are more than disposable beings in our increasingly youth-obsessed ...

documentary like this. It's a gorgeous, hilarious, sad, wonderful, unblinking look at the joy of life — even at the end of it.

We meet and live with the folks at Harbor Place along with young Jenks. Like any society, Harbor Place has its funny people ...

lege boy? Boy, are you in trouble!")

When he glances at the bag she's holding from the drug store, she says: "I just picked up my birth control pills!"

Then there's Bill Delarm, an 80-year old who wears a different Hawaiian ...

and his cameraman walked the halls bringing comfort and help to residents who were running out of oxygen. Terrifying.

At other times, some residents discuss how unfortunate it is that, in the US, we don't ...

Andrew Jenks, Room 335
"A LOVELY AND GENUINE ACCOUNT OF GENERATIONAL UNDERSTANDING!"
-Variety

into a world that's usually invisible and shines a light on a population that many of us would just soon forget."

—*The New York Times*

"It's almost impossible to believe that a kid could produce a documentary like this. It's a gorgeous, hilarious, sad, wonderful, unblinking look at the joy of life—even at the end of it."

—*The New York Post*

"HBO is fine, kid. But unless you make the next *My Big Fat *@%&* Greek Wedding*, this will be your first and last film."

And that was my introduction to the seamy side of Hollywood, of agents with dollar signs in their eyes, chasing a kid with a good review in *Variety*. I was nineteen and didn't care how much some Ari Gold wannabe told me off.

In this ruthless industry, I realized, I'd have to accept people yelling that I was a nobody.

I was back at NYU (which didn't get any better after spending six weeks in a nursing home, making a documentary, and getting accepted at a few film festivals), lying on my bed and mulling over the problems of a sophomore, when my cell rang. The area code was 212. No one I knew had a 212 area code. It was all 917, 718, or 347. The 212 was official. I picked up right away.

"This is John Hoffman from HBO," the voice on the other end said. "We want to buy your movie."

Holy cow, HBO wants to buy my movie! This is everyone's dream!

This is my dream.

I can't believe it. How in the hell did this happen?

Every time I went to HBO and they gave me a pass, I kept it. HBO buying my doc never got old. It still isn't.

"HBO's interested, huh?" I said in my best this-is-not-a-big-deal voice. "That's cool. Can I get your number and call you back in five minutes?"

"Excuse me?"

"You know, it's just that a lot of people have called," I said. "I need to talk to my lawyer and figure out how to push this properly."

"Totally understand," John said. "Totally."

I hung up the phone, and suddenly realized I had no idea what I was doing. I did what I always do when I'm in that position: I called my dad. After I explained the situation to him and asked how I should handle it, he said, for the first time in my life, "I have no clue."

So I went to my second-best source, the Internet. I looked up "TV lawyers" and found someone who helped me sell *Room 335* to HBO, which ended up playing it all over the country and then all over the world.

My first kiss.
Damn...

I boarded the plane returning home from Dallas, where HBO had screened my film. As I walked to my seat I noticed a woman about my age sitting toward the back. As I approached her seat I kept doing the math, trying to figure out if my seat was next to hers. Sure enough, it was.

I sat down and was immediately in love. I pretended to tie my shoe so that I could see who her book's author was. As I sat back, I told her I liked her taste in literature.

"I love that author," I said. "That's his new book, right?"

She looked at me like I was crazy.

"He's been dead for thirty years."

I quickly brought up another book, which she knew—nice save—and we wound up talking for the entire flight. She was in advertising. She liked basketball. Her favorite TV show was *The West Wing*. This was meant to be. We were about to land when I got bold and asked her out to dinner when we arrived in New York. She said yes.

Before we went out, we had a few drinks at my place. At which point, I realized something really bad. **I never got her name.**

Maybe in the first few moments back in Dallas, but that was hours ago. Yes, I was in love, but so in love, I forgot the only thing I really had to know. While she was in the bathroom, I grabbed her purse to look at her wallet and get her name. Big mistake.

Premiering the film in Australia (above) and Europe (below)

When she walked out and caught me snooping in her purse, she did exactly what I would have done: **got the hell out of there.**

My Dallas love was short-lived. For the next few weeks, though, I did my best to relive our flight-long romance. I wrote a movie script about it.

I returned to Harbor Place with my mom, because she had fallen in love with some of the characters she'd seen in *Room 335*. I decided to screen the movie there as an excuse for the visit. I showed it to Tammy and Libby, and we're not ten minutes into the film when Tammy interrupts: "Can you fast-forward to the parts we're in? We don't really have time for this. We live this every day."

"Bingo starts in an hour," Libby added.

So I did just what they asked, and they were really happy.

"We look so great," Tammy said. "This is fabulous."

Even for the reunion, Jonah felt obligated to film.

"Let's go play bingo," Libby said.

They didn't care about the cameras. Or that the movie was playing around the world. In fact, when the *Daily News* called Libby to interview her, she hung up the phone. A publicist told me this and I quickly called Libby.

"Why did you hang up on the *Daily News*?" I asked.
"You can't trust those gossip papers," she said.

I convinced Libby to talk to the reporter, who had loved the movie, and she agreed. But, she said, only because I asked.

Later that night, my mom and I showed it to Bill, who sat through all ninety minutes, much to my gratification. When I asked him what he thought, he asked,
"Who's the woman who has been sitting next to me the whole time?"
"That's my mom."
"She divorced?"
"You know, Bill, I put my blood, sweat, and tears into this movie," I said. "Did you even watch it?"

Bill shrugged. "Your mom is really good-looking."

chapter five

BE MY VALENTINE?

千葉ロッテマリーンズ
ご声援
ありがとう!!
千葉ロッテマリーンズ
クライマックスシリーズ
第2ステージ進出決定!!
もれなく
500円お買い上げごとに、
100円のクーポン券をプレゼント!
キャッシュバック
クーポンプレゼント!
2
キャンペーン期間
10/5～11/7まで
LOTTERIA
RECAP

How the hell was I going to find Bobby Valentine?

Back during my freshman year, when I needed a break from my search for a senior citizen home that would accept me as a resident, I decided to Google Bobby Valentine to see what the former baseball manager was up to (cyberstalking to find cool documentary subjects is a favorite procrastination technique). He took a terrible Mets team to the World Series in 2000. What happened? Well, a lot. He'd gone to Japan to revitalize the sport for a country that was crazy for baseball. I realized Bobby V.'s story was a tailor-made documentary film. But I was in the middle of chasing one film most people didn't think I could make. I couldn't really start another.

Once I returned from the whirlwind tour with *Room 335*, I went with Jonah and another NYU student, Andrew Muscato, to Pennsylvania. We were documenting a professional rugby team where all of the players were also teachers at a juvenile detention center. Muscato had an in at ESPN, so as we wrapped filming, we pitched the idea to the network. They quickly said no. But before we left the meeting, I brought up Bobby V. As I explained to the ESPN producer in my pitch, Bobby V. was treated like a god in Japan. The movie would be *Lost in Translation* meets *Mr. Baseball* as we'd follow his strange life as a cult sports figure in a totally foreign culture. ESPN was interested.

I thought it was brilliant, but you never know what other people are going to think. Then I got the call. "We really like this idea," an ESPN exec said. "Can you and Bobby come in next week?"

"Sure, no problem," I said.

I've always loved playing sports. It gets my mind away from everything.

Bobby V. was famously thrown out of a game, but couldn't resist managing. So he came back in with a Groucho Marx outfit.

But there was a problem. I had no idea how to get in touch with Bobby V. So I went straight to the Internet. I searched for an agent or email address. Not surprisingly, I came up empty-handed. Famous people don't exactly like to put their personal information on the Web.

I started randomly emailing different addresses that I thought could be his.

All I got in return were delivery error messages and replies like:

"I'm a plumber from Kansas, you jackass."
"I'm not *that* Bobby V."
"You can't scam me."

I was getting desperate. If I had to tell ESPN that I didn't know how to get in contact with Bobby V., I really was going to look like a jackass.

While describing my rapidly approaching crisis to Zinn, the same guy who had filmed me getting harassed by the pizza guys, he remembered that his mom had some connection to Bobby V. In an incredible stroke of luck, Linda did know one of his relatives and got me his email address.

I emailed Bobby and he wrote back to meet him Sunday at his bar, Bobby Valentine's Sports Gallery Cafe in Stamford, Connecticut, where he claims to have invented the wrap—apparently his restaurant was the first anywhere to serve a sandwich wrapped in a tortilla.

Jonah and I drove with Muscato to Bobby V.'s Sports Gallery Cafe and sat down on a couple of bar stools, ordered soda, and waited until, finally, he came out. Face-to-face with a baseball legend, I did my best to exude confidence as I explained that we wanted to follow him around in Japan for nine months. When he took over the Chiba Lotte Marines in 2003, the team hadn't won a series in thirty-one years. Within two years, he'd taken the major league Bad News Bears and turned them into national champions in both the Japan and Asia Series.

American viewers would be riveted, I continued, by a story about the intersection of Bobby, baseball, and Japanese culture.

"Absolutely no way," Bobby said. "There's a Japanese saying that if a nail sticks out, you hammer it back down. I'm kind of already that nail. I don't need three American teenagers to follow me around with a camera to make it worse."

Jonah, Me, Muscato, and Bobby at his bar

Sitting in the ESPN offices, I saw eight guys in suits go into the conference room for my meeting. *Our meeting.*

After three hours of talking to Bobby V. that day in Connecticut, we convinced him to take the meeting. Well, maybe it was more that Bobby decided to take a chance on us. Chances, in general, are something he likes. He's never said it, but I think in that bar, he looked at us—three measly college students who had a fantasy—and realized that sitting in front of him was everything he loved about the world. There's no bigger dreamer than Bobby.

I looked at the suits filing past us; these guys were serious. They were running ESPN, the worldwide leader in sports. A channel most of us grew up on. I looked at Bobby, "the brightest mind in baseball." Then I thought about myself. The meeting hadn't even begun yet, and I already started to see it play out. Bobby would tear the house down with his stories. The ESPN guys would love him. And then they were going to look at me and my buddies and think, "This is a great story. Bobby V. is killer, but who is this guy that made some movie about old people?"

I took Bobby aside and was straight with him. At some point in the conversation, I needed him to say he'd only make this movie with the three of us.

KOREA
TOWN
KIPS
BAY

There was a beer, a hamburger, and a street named after him. When a poll was taken asking the Japanese who, in an ideal world, they would want their boss to be, the answer was Bobby V.

"I've only known you for a week, kid," he said. "Why would I say that?"

"Because I'm the one who came up with the idea, and the three of us will live in Japan for nine months to get it right," I said. "Look, they may find you some other director, who might be a star, but he'll fly in and fly out once a month. He'll be in it for the money and not much else. I'll be there for every game, every inning, every damn pitch. This actually means the world to me."

My paranoia was kicking in hard.

"I'll think about it."

A shrine where visitors came for good luck

The meeting went pretty much just as I'd expected any meeting to go with Bobby. He had the ESPN execs riveted with his stories of the high life in Japan. The same way I drooled when reading his story years ago.

"Oh my God, there's a burger named after you? Fellas, can you believe that?"
"I want a BoBeer."
"You can park in the middle of the highway and won't even get a ticket?"

I didn't really say much. The meeting was about to wrap up—the executives were telling Bobby all the great moments they loved about his career—and my name still hadn't come up. So I looked over at Bobby to nudge him.

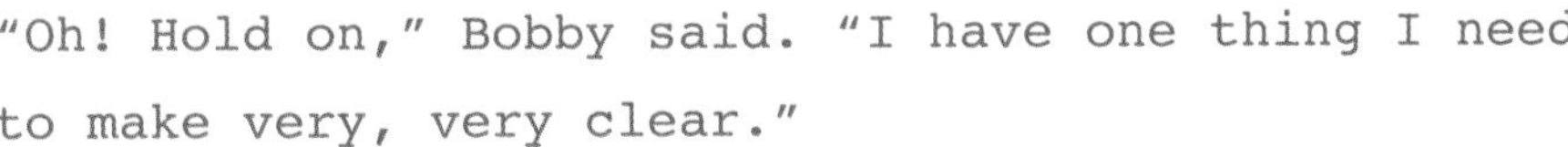
"Oh! Hold on," Bobby said. "I have one thing I need to make very, very clear."

The men all paid careful attention. This was the moment when I realized what made a leader, or a coach at least. It was someone who can make the whole room pay attention, as if his every word had life-altering consequences.

They took their pens and notepads back out.

"Yes, Bobby?" Bobby looked at them, one by one, in the eye, almost uncomfortably, and said, "Listen, I will not make this movie unless it's directed by Andrew *Jerks*."

Oh boy.

"*Jenks*, Bobby. *Jenks*," I said.
"Right. Sorry. Jenks, Jonah, and Muscato. These are the three."

A few months later, I woke up in the middle of the night with my tooth killing me. I knew something was really wrong, so I waited until the morning and took the train upstate to see my dentist, who pulled my wisdom teeth out, put me in a ton of pain, made me unable to chew, and knocked me out on drugs.

Back in my childhood bedroom, unable to eat anything other than ice cream, I watched the entire first season of *Brothers & Sisters* on the Internet. My "office," where I had edited *Internal Injustice*, was papered in posters of old movies no one had ever heard of. During high school, I would always go to the local movie-rental place and ask them for posters they were planning to throw out and salvage them for my lair. As I lay reminiscing in bed, I was already dreading returning to school.

Pain included, this was a vacation from junior year, which was worse than major dental surgery. The only thing good about my life in New York was my

Back at home, watching old footage on VideoWave III

new apartment. That fall, in addition to my annual dread of starting school, I also found out that Bill and Tammy died. I had called Harbor Place to tell Tammy that I was sending them our latest film festival trophy and I learned that she'd passed away not long after Bill. I hadn't known what it was like for friends to die. I cried for a long time. And then cried some more. I went to Bill's funeral a week later. So did Jonah and Will. We met his family. We spent time in their home, looking at old pictures and hearing some of their favorite Bill stories.

After that, I couldn't stand the closet that Jonah and I called our apartment. A block away from Washington Square Park, it was only a small hallway with no real rooms or windows, just bunk beds and a small bathroom that was in the kitchen—a smelly combo. So I took the money from selling *Room 335* to HBO and splurged on a nicer place on Mulberry and Prince. There was a bookstore across the street where they had free Internet, and a famous graveyard on the corner that was used in a Scorsese film. It was a perfect New York City location.

The area I lived in right before moving to Japan

Still, I preferred recuperating at home, far from New York City, in a modest house surrounded by trees . . . the suburbs.

In bed, I watched Nora and Kitty get into it over Justin's decision to go back into the army when the phone rang.

Area code 212.

I picked up.

It was John Dahl and Dan Silver, executive producers at ESPN, calling to tell me that the Bobby V. movie had been greenlit. The quick, direct conversation left me stunned. I kind of went into a daze that I don't think had anything to do with all the painkillers I was taking. Starting in the beginning of the school year, we'd had so many meetings with the sports network, and I could never tell what they were thinking. As it turned out, ESPN was going to give us somewhere around a million dollars to make this movie—about one million more than it cost to make my first movie.

One million dollars.

Whenever I get good news, I always take a moment to enjoy it on my own. ESPN's news was crazy good, life-changing, I'm-going-to-Japan-for-nine-months-to-make-a-million-dollar-movie good, so I lay on my bed for a long while, savoring the moment before it was tainted with anything real.

I walked downstairs, went into the living room, where my dad was watching TV, and lay down on the crummy old white sofa with a huge grin on my face.

"What?" My dad asked.
"ESPN is going to pay for the movie."

He gave me a serious look to see if I was serious. His face was stunned. Then he pivoted in his chair and grinned. There's no better feeling than making my dad proud. One of the first things he said was something I will never forget.

"Someone else has now given you money to make a movie," my dad said. "This is real."

I hadn't thought about it like that, but my dad was right. This was real.

Even though it was nice, I never went back to that apartment on Prince Street (Jonah grabbed my clothes and my *Lost* DVDs, which was all I had)—or school. I was going to Japan for nine months. I was getting paid to make a movie. I was a filmmaker. Officially, though, I dropped out of NYU on a toothache.

chapter six

I'M FAMOUS IN JAPAN

I stepped on board. Off to Tokyo, Japan. By myself.

I was going to meet everyone and check out Japan until Muscato and Jonah flew over a few weeks later with all the equipment. I felt a difference in culture from the moment I buckled my seat belt. The Japan Airlines flight attendant handed me a hot towel, smiling and offering a tiny bow of respect. I was used to being treated like cattle in the air, not like a VIP.

Fourteen hours later, I was in a car with the fast-talking Larry Rocca, a friend and business associate of Bobby's. He gave me a 101 on Japan en route to the hotel:

Everyone is really nice.
They work really hard.
They take tremendous pride in their country.
The girls love Americans.

He was nice enough to check me into the APA Hotel, fifty floors of cold steel and glass sticking straight up into the sky. This anonymous tower, in the middle of the otherwise low-lying Chiba suburbs, forty-five miles west of Tokyo near the stadium, would be home base for the better part of a year.

Right: The APA Hotel literally looked over the stadium.
Above: Our view from the 42nd floor.

Checking audio levels over and over again

"Andrew" is tough to say for the Japanese, so for eight months, I went only by Andy-San, meaning "Mr. Andy."

On my first night, I went to a local restaurant and got a table in the corner. I spread out all of my books, papers, and studying materials on Japan and baseball. I knew I had a lot to learn, not so much about the game, but the culture. I looked at the menu and realized I was at an Italian restaurant. So I studied Japanese culture while eating a bowl of spaghetti and red sauce (later this became my favorite restaurant and I ended up going back nearly a hundred times. They served the best bowl of spaghetti I have ever had anywhere). I returned to my room and wrote my mom.

From:
To:
Cc:
Sent: Thu, 15 Mar 2007 5:33 AM
Subject: Re: hi!

HEY MOM I CANT FIGURE OUT HOW TO TYPE ON THESE JAPAN TYPING BOARDS ITS REALLY REAALY WEIRD BUT I LL FIGURE IT OUT THIS PLACE IS AWESEOME VERY VERY COOL INCREDIBLY CLEAN I HAVE AN AMAZING VIEWOF THE BAY FROM MY HOTEL AND LARRY ROCCA IS REALLY COOL....HE SAYS ALL THREE OF US WILL FALL IN LOVE BY TGE TIME THIS IS OVER,,,,ANYWAY ALL IS GOING REALLY WELL FLIGHT WAS FINE I LL EMAIL TOMORROW WHEN I CAN SEND SOMETHING THAT MAKES SENSE ,,,,THIS MOVIE IS GOING TO BE REALLY REALLY REALLY GOOD

From:
Date: Thu, Mar 15, 2007 at 7:04 AM
Subject: Re: hi!
To:

You've just made my morning! I am so glad that so far, so good. It sounds wonderful! Daddy and I were thinking about you non-stop and hoping the arrival went ok. Get some sleep - and look sharp in your new clothes when you meet the players! Don't forget how to hand our your cards! (just kidding).
Love you...xxxxMom and Dad

The irony wasn't lost on me. Someone who basically panicked about going away to college an hour from home had pitched making a movie seven thousand miles away. Maybe I didn't think ESPN would ever go for it. Maybe I just didn't think. But before I left for Japan, I worried about living so far away from home. Would I get any sleep during the next nine months?

Thank God for work.

After a lonely first night, the next morning I went to the Chiba Marines baseball stadium. Walking to the stadium, I still felt very far from home, even though I passed a Starbucks, McDonald's, Outback, you name it. Once in the stadium, I felt even more out of my element. I'm usually the guy way up in the bleachers, and here I was walking right out onto the field of the thirty-thousand-seat stadium. As a huge sports fan and human being aware of special circumstances, I was in awe. Bobby, whom I hadn't seen since the ESPN meeting, came up and patted me on the back. With a smirk on his face, he said, "So you showed up alone with no film crew and no equipment? You sure ESPN said yes?"

That was just the beginning.

Famous Koshien Stadium

専修大学
(03)
3265
5973

Kidding around before our trip up Fuji—I had no idea what I was in for. Twelve hours later I was on top—shaking because I was freezing and rain was all over, my body depleted. Jonah did the same thing—but with a camera. Bobby called it the most athletic performance he'd ever seen.

People always ask me what Japan is like. My answer is: I am not sure I really know.

Although I visited every big city and small town, ate every kind of specialty and local food, and tried to understand the language and customs, I was traveling with the most recognizable guy in Japan. His face was plastered on huge billboards. He had a beer named after him. If a foreigner traveled across the U.S. with Brad Pitt for almost a year, I am not so sure what they'd make of America.

So what was Japan like? Surreal.

Speeding all over the country in bullet trains and planes, we ate Korean barbecue with the Backstreet Boys of Japan one night and did karaoke in a $2,000-an-hour private room with multibillionaires the next night. And when we weren't right next to Bobby, we were hanging out or traveling with players who were almost as famous. Everywhere we went in the small country, people turned their heads.

Me, Muscato, and Bobby in the dugout before a game

Famous shrine in Kyoto
Top Right: Me taking a break from Japanese food after a long day. Not Jonah.
Bottom Right: My transportation to work (the stadium)

My grandfather, with Eleanor Roosevelt, at the time of the adoption of the Universal Declaration on Human Rights in 1948. My grandfather was also a prolific author and a world-renowned international lawyer.

One evening we dined in Osaka at the U.S. consulate's house, surrounded by dignitaries. Before I had left for Japan, my grandmother had sent me a large golden key with "Osaka" written on it. My father's father, who died long before I was born and had been director general of the International Labour Organization, knew people all over the world—including in the city of Osaka. Forty years earlier, he was honored with the key to the city, which I threw into my bag without much thought before I left for Japan.

I carried it in my back pocket that night and showed it to the consulate and the Japanese dignitaries. Some looked shocked. Others had tears in their eyes. Japan is such a proud nation. Watching a young American in Osaka produce this key really meant something to them.

My grandmother, J.J., Dad, my brother, me, and Mom at ceremony for my grandfather

As we toasted to the grandfather I never met, I reflected on my life. I'm twenty-one, toasting top government officials and eating Kobe beef, the best in the world.

We later learned the beef was actually American, which particularly disgusted Bobby. I returned to our hotel and immediately called my grandmother J.J. (Jane Jenks), who never liked being called "grandmother" because it sounded too old. In my hotel room with a triangular ceiling, oddly colored yellow walls, and a view of the parking lot, I told her what had happened. An eighty-two-year-old woman who lost her husband thirty-two years earlier, J.J. talked about my grandfather like she had seen him yesterday. It was my happiest moment in Japan. And it may be my favorite phone call I ever had—even above all those ones from 212.

HOTEL

With Bobby, we were always moving and seeing and meeting. Keeping up with Bobby was not easy, even for three 21-year-olds. I've never met someone as energetic. If *Room 335* was about slowing down my metabolism so that I could spend all day playing bingo, then documenting Bobby was the exact opposite. It was in Japan that I started drinking coffee for the first time, enormous cups of Starbucks's bitterly caffeinated coffee.

The baseball season was 162 games and nonstop traveling for seven months. It was grueling. A day off was something we looked forward to for weeks. For Bobby, though, a day off was an excuse to do something ridiculous, like:

- Giving inspirational speeches to companies, colleges, you name it, where people acted like the Pope was talking.
- Eating pizza with Tommy Lasorda or a steak with Nolan Ryan.
- Traveling to Hawaii for a couple days.
- Skiing on a closed mountain a few hours north of Sapporo.
- Climbing Fuji.
- Going to a rock concert where the crowd erupted and began chanting his name as soon as they realized he was backstage.
- Standing on the top of a house to watch Kyoto's fire festival.

Bobby exploring a park the morning before a night game. He said it was his chance to think about what order to place batters, which relief pitches to use, and also a "time to just think."

We went wherever Bobby went, which was everywhere—including on the bike rides he took all the time. We had to import a tandem bike from Hawaii that either Andrew Muscato or I rode with Jonah in the back, filming. While we had used wheelchairs for cool tracking shots in *Room 335*, for *Bobby V.* we used a combination of bikes, convertibles, and skis.

Bobby didn't just invite us everywhere to be nice to the guys making the movie (in fact, he didn't seem to care all that much about the movie; sometimes I wonder if he ever actually saw it).

He let us tag around, because he wanted us to learn about Japanese culture (though, much like the residents in *Room 335*, he enjoyed the company more than anything else). When we chose the Outback Steakhouse over Japanese food (there's only so much Korean barbecue and sushi you can eat), he was pissed. "You're eating that?" he said, as if we were breaking his heart.

Me in Hiroshima, after dozens of students surrounded Bobby for autographs. You can see the "Atomic Dome" behind me, the closest surviving building to the location of the nuclear bomb.

But whenever Bobby taught us about Japanese culture, I was more struck by his place within it. While in Hiroshima, where the Allies dropped one of two atomic bombs on Japan during World War II, he took us to the area of the bombing, which is now a historical monument to the event. While we stood on this site of historical atrocity, thirty Japanese kids in yellow hats abandoned their school tour to swarm Bobby in excitement. For the next hour or so, he signed autographs for smiling children in the heart of the nation's greatest tragedy.

Jonah the Assassin

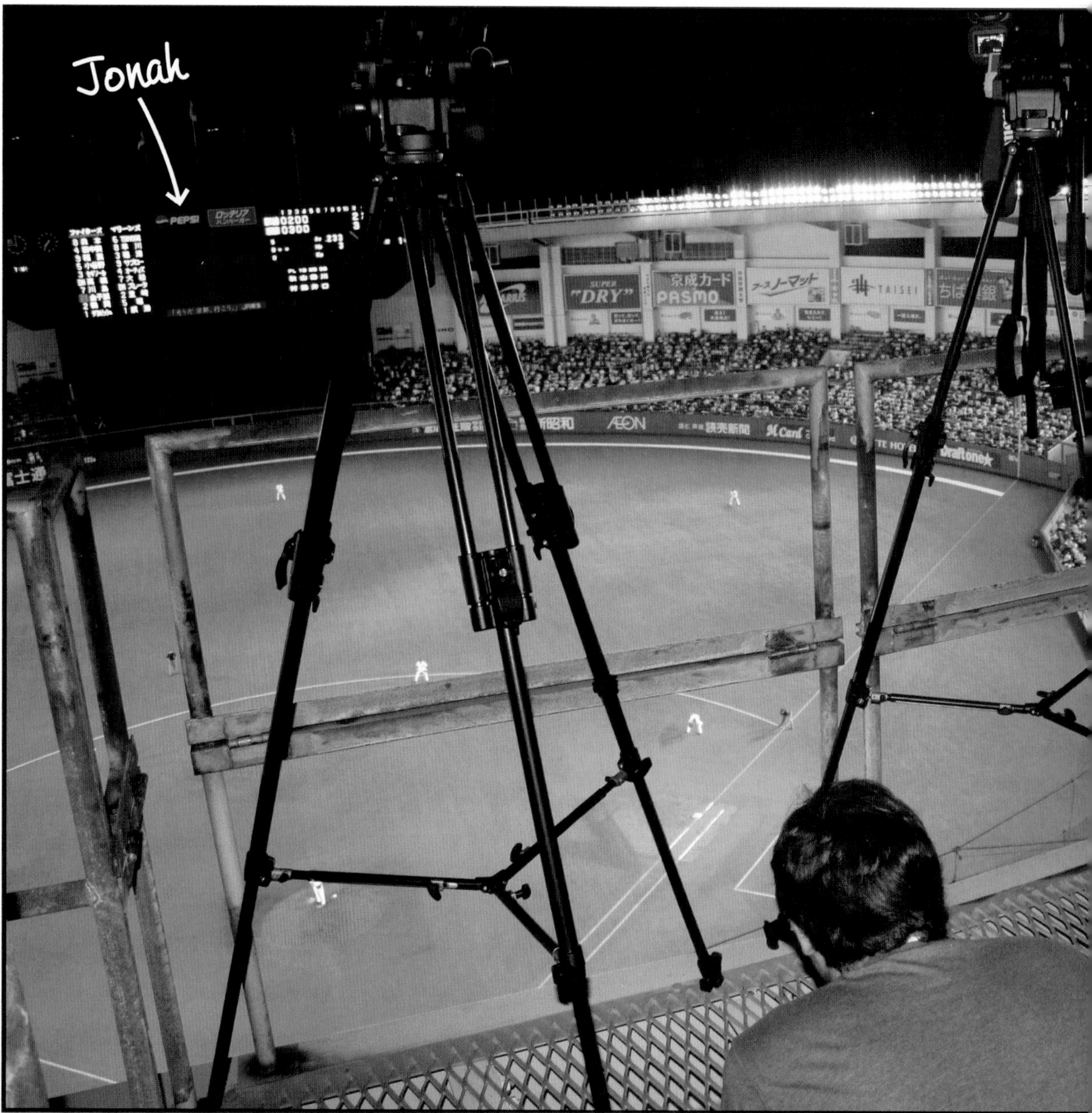

On top of the stadium, shooting, but without Tokyo in the background. That's why we always wanted to be on top of that scoreboard.

It was game three of the climax series and possibly the last for Bobby's Chiba Lotte Marines. Either they won and moved on, or they lost and the season was over.

It was the eighth inning, with two outs to go, when Jonah approached me and Muscato in the pressroom: "Dude, we got to get *that* shot."

The shot he was talking about was one from on top of the scoreboard with the baseball game in the foreground and sweeping views of Tokyo, forty miles south, just behind. We knew we wanted that shot in the movie from the minute we stepped into the stadium, but Bobby had said unequivocally and on many occasions, "Absolutely not."

"We can't go," I said to Jonah. "We just can't do it."

"I don't know, man. It's now or never. What's the worst that's going to happen? They tell us off?"

"I guess so."

Once Jonah has an idea in his head, there's not much point in arguing with him. So off he went, carrying his tripod in his backpack like some modern-day Robin Hood.

About twenty minutes later, while I was eating some salmon sushi (really, really good salmon sushi), there was a commotion in the media area. All these Japanese reporters were gathered together around the TV monitor, whispering to each other. I found one who spoke English and asked what was going on.

"There's a foreign sniper on top of the scoreboard trying to kill everyone!" he said. "They're evacuating the stadium."

"What the hell are you talking about?"

I moved through the group of people to get a look at the TV screen, which wasn't showing the game or the score. It was a big frontal shot of Jonah sitting there with a huge smile on his face like, "Yeah, I'm getting the shot, I'm getting the shot."

Left: When not filming, we spent hours in the media room. Right: Jonah making up with police a few days later. Not sure they're the same ones . . .

Time to freak out.

I sprinted in a panic to the dugout to find Bobby, the only person in the country who could possibly keep Jonah from getting a bullet in his forehead by a Japanese SWAT team. As I was running, I looked up into the stands, which were packed for the biggest game of the season, and saw that no one was evacuating. In fact, the crowd looked like it was doing the wave. I knew the Japanese were baseball nuts, but this was insane. Then I realized they weren't doing the wave. It seemed like every time time Jonah panned the shot with the tripod, the section of the stadium he faced hit the ground.

When I finally arrived at the dugout, Bobby was steaming, red-faced mad.

"It's Jonah, isn't it?" he growled.

The authorities got Jonah down in one piece and left him that way (I had convinced them he was a confused teenager). Jonah probably has already forgotten this story. But what he certainly does remember is that he got the shot.

During a trip to Kobe my grandfather died; the same grandfather who had inspired my first movie and, ultimately, led me to this adventure of a lifetime.

Married for 57 years. Grandad would always look at Nana like this.

I was in my hotel room when my mom called.

"He's not doing well," she said.
"I'm coming home."
"It's okay, Andrew. Your brother and cousins aren't here. Grandad would want you guys to be out there making him proud."

My grandmother got on the phone and repeated what my mom said: It was just her, my mom, and my aunt. I went to sleep and woke up the next morning, knowing that he was gone before my mom had called to confirm it. The guys came by to pick me up to go to the local stadium, like we did every day, except that day I didn't go. After I told them about my grandfather, they expressed their condolences and then left me alone in my hotel room.

Only days before I was on top of the world. But as I sat in the hotel room I felt far from it. Traveling with Japanese icons, millionaires, and pop stars became unbearably lonely. Thanksgiving dinner with Jonah and the other Andrew in the hotel where they shot *Lost in Translation* was surreal. Alone in some random hotel room in the middle of the night, I tortured myself with the idea that I wasn't doing anything productive and no one would care even if I were. *A movie about Japanese baseball?*

On the road, a lot goes on with no outlet in which to express it. Everyone around me was someone I worked with, someone who had invested in me—even Bobby. I couldn't dump on them or worry them about my state of mind. So I internalized my grief, walking around Kobe, listening to ESPN podcasts for comfort, and stopping every now and then to sit down on a bench and cry.

But I kept going. Mainly because I believed in our movie.

Bobby's self-awareness of his intelligence is partly where he draws the confidence for his favorite role: champion of the underdog. There's nothing he likes better than to save the day. He takes players that most people see as throwaway, like overweight right fielder Benny Agbayani, who helped bring the Mets to the World Series, and makes them part of his team.

Bobby trying to enjoy the cherry blossoms in Sendai...quickly surrounded by adoring fans

At the top of the stands before a game. All good, Jonah was filming the grass growing.

When somebody asked him to call a kid who lost his dad on 9/11, Bobby knocked on the kid's house in Brooklyn that very night. He sat down to dinner with the family and to this day hasn't stopped acting like a dad to that kid.

Bobby brought rooting for the underdog to a level I didn't even know was possible. He embraced people whom everyone else had overlooked. When he found hidden potential, that's when Bobby got going. "You are an average baseball player," he might say. "But I'm going to sign you and make this work." He set out to prove that discounting anyone was wrong. And I admired him immensely, because he succeeded.

Very late in the night, Jonah checking out the latest cut at the apartment, downtown in the Financial District.

chapter seven

MTV COMES TO MY BEDROOM

I was first introduced to Hollywood after *Room 335* aired. I got calls from a lot of people in the business and flew out to Los Angeles to sign with a sleazy agent. Staying at the house of a friend whose parents had a lot of money, I spent most of my time by the pool. In the end, that's basically all that came of it.

After *The Zen of Bobby V.* came out, things really started to happen. It was everything *Internal Injustice* was meant to be. First there was the film opening at the Tribeca Film Festival. While I was still at NYU, the festival would roll around and all you'd hear about were the greatest films and coolest stars being in town for it. Started as a way to revitalize Lower Manhattan after September 11, Tribeca had turned into one of the hottest festivals in the country—and I was, unbelievably, invited. The days of walking the streets with postcards and living in a motel forty miles away from the action were gone. I was at the opening-night party with James Gandolfini, Jerry Seinfeld, Anjelica Huston, Harvey Weinstein, Robert De Niro, Lorne Michaels, Billy Crystal, my favorite character from *Boy Meets World*...and Spike Lee.

At Foreign Press Center in New York City for a press conference with Bobby streaming live from Japan

FOREIGN PRESS CENTER
NEW YORK

"Hey, Spike," I said.

"Yo," he replied, refusing to look me in the eye. I didn't care. He's a Knicks fan, so it was all good.

"Just wanted to say love all of your movies, man, *BIG* fan. I know you're busy. . . ."

"I am busy."

"I know you dig sports. I have this sports doc playing tomorrow night on Third Avenue."

"Sorry man. I'm busy."

"Cool. Well, okay . . . take care."

"Yeah."

Spike might not have been interested, but with one film on HBO and another on ESPN, multiple big-time talent agencies were. I got a lot of wild pitches.

"Anderson Cooper is leaving *The Mole*," said one agent at a small Midtown Manhattan bar. "You could be the next host." That was the funniest thing I'd heard in a while.

Then I met the agent to end all agents.

"Come to the top of the Gramercy Park Hotel. Just say you know Frank."

"But your name isn't Frank."

Audible sigh.

"Just say you know Frank."

Promoting the film

LANCÔME

At a shoot in TriBeCa

In the elevator going to the rooftop—oh snap—there was Matt Damon. It's funny when people say they don't care about seeing famous people in real life. I couldn't disagree more. It's weird to see someone on a screen and then in person. The important thing is not to stare so much that it gets creepy. I snuck a few glances at the actor, but in an elevator it's hard to be discreet. Exiting out onto the top floor, I smelled beauty. Well-placed roses, plush seats, expensive rugs. I was escorted to a private room. There the agent, Adam Berkowitz, and a top-flight business manager, David Levin, stood up.

With the city glittering at his back, Berkowitz crossed his legs and launched right in:

"Listen, you've made two movies and you're only 21. The sky's the limit. CAA is the best agency in Hollywood. We just are. And I want to sign you so that you can do whatever you want."

That sounded great, of course, but what won me over was the generosity he lavished on three scrubby guys. He had us over in a private room with the best bottle of wine. And unlike the other agents who acted like they were doing us a favor, he made it clear that this deal would be good for all of us. We ended up flying to Los Angeles, where he and his team drove us around Hollywood. We walked around famous studio lots and old film sets, the same ones I had visited years earlier as a tourist, dreaming that one day I could make it. I didn't feel at all like I had made it, I still don't, but the trip was nice.

Around the same time, I received a random email from MTV saying they were interested in having a meeting. Strange. But cool.

I wasn't sure exactly where I would fit in among programs like *Jersey Shore* and *16 and Pregnant*. I'm not really that proud of my abs. I certainly wasn't pregnant.

How could I make myself appealing to a super pop-culture network like MTV?

Everyone has a story and telling those stories is what I do. But I needed to find a story to interest a younger audience. I didn't sweat it too much though. My friends all know this about me; I manage expectations pretty well. While I go into any meeting really, really prepared and convinced that mine is the smartest idea the people I'm pitching to could do, I simultaneously psych myself out by deciding that it'll still never ever happen.

When I sat down at the network's headquarters (the same building where *TRL* was shot) with about fifteen executives from MTV, including everyone in charge of programming, I was sure this wasn't going to happen. But I gave it my best shot.

"What if I moved in with a rapper?" I proposed.

Rap Jenks Rap would be a full season of a rapper and me. I couldn't gauge the reaction of the room. The most senior exec seemingly ignored my pitch and just kept asking me about what it was like to live in a nursing home.

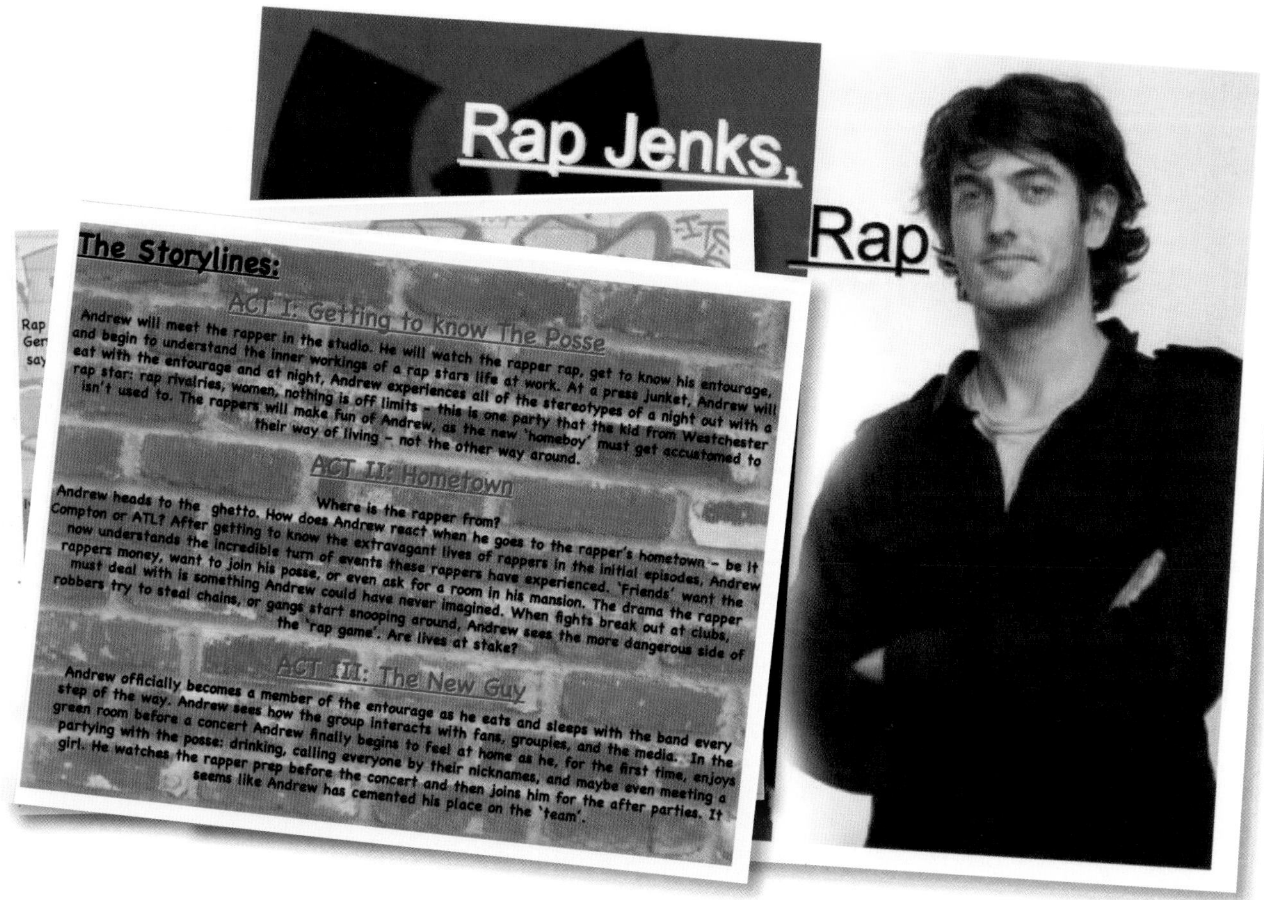

Amazingly, they went for it enough to give me fifty thousand dollars to make a five-minute sizzle reel. The chances were slim, but if the execs loved what they saw on the reel they might give me a shot at a show.

I don't really believe in presentations. I just want to get in the room.

I didn't waste the 50K, but my approach didn't have a lot to do with the MTV show.

I used some of it to pay late rent and most of it to produce what I expected to be a ninety-minute documentary about a rapper (in my MTV contract, I retained the rights to the footage if they didn't pick up the show idea, which was the most likely scenario).

I started looking for a rapper who'd let me move into his home. For months, I cold-called managers. It didn't matter if I dropped the name MTV or my new agency, Creative Arts Agency (Andrew Jenks definitely didn't get me anywhere), everyone blew me off. Eventually I called Berkowitz and owned up to the fact that after three whole months of trying, I had nothing to show for it. He called me back within five minutes.

"I know the guy who runs rap in New York City," he said. "You're meeting with him."

And within days, I met Maino.

Ah, Maino.

When I first met him, he instantly reminded me of Bobby V. He had that presence. Surrounded by record-label executives, a huge radio station owner, and someone else important looking, Maino listened to my pitch and then took a strong minute to think.

"I got one problem with this idea."

Usually, one problem is harder than a lot of problems. Because one problem means it's usually *huge*, and there are no conditions.

I looked over at J.J., who I brought along because he happened to be in town. I figured Maino would have an entourage, so I'd bring my own version. J.J., looking like my agent in a fairly nice suit, didn't say anything. It was pretty badass that my agent didn't say a word.

Getting a word in with Maino isn't always easy.

Finally Maino broke the silence.

"My one problem is I don't understand how I didn't come up with this idea myself."

Everyone laughed. Maino was in.

Maino had a different girl in every city, a hard-partying crew, and a penchant for taking off his shirt, but he really worked. No manufactured product of a label's marketing exec, he was hood. Born in Bedford-Stuyvesant, Brooklyn, to parents who both wound up on drugs, he had been left to fend for himself and his younger brother, while still barely a teen.

Proving to Maino I could hang and wasn't, as he said, just some kid "from the 'burbs, where there are cul-de-sacs."

That led to a life of crime, which led to ten years in jail for kidnapping. "We grabbed some guy, put him in a van, and just kind of took him," he told me. "And, well, kinda forgot to give him back."

Maino looked at me casually, almost like not returning a person after taking him isn't a big deal. A big part of my job is reading faces, understanding when people are down to open up and when they're not. As I questioned why he did that and how being locked up for ten years changed him, Maino's face let me know that he wasn't down to say anything more than his flippant line about forgetting some guy in a van. He wasn't ready.

First we had to go on a crazy ride with him.

Maino never slowed down his life for me. When we followed him to Atlanta for T.I.'s going-away-to-jail concert, Maino took a private security escort to

the concert while Jonah and I followed behind in our rental car. His driver slapped a siren on top of the black vehicle and quickly hit 120 miles per hour. Maino was not the type of guy to make sure we were behind him. He definitely had no idea this concert was going to be a key part of the story. We had to catch him.

So there we were, in a midsize economy car barreling down some Atlanta highway at twice the speed limit, weaving in and out of terrified traffic, trying not to die . . . Or flying over the Venetian Causeway in Miami by using the lane reserved for emergency vehicles, so that we didn't have to sit in traffic . . . Or getting past about ten velvet ropes so that we were in the V.V.V.I.P. section of the hottest club . . . Or hanging out in the stairwell of a housing project surrounded by his boys in Bed-Stuy. Maino didn't care. "Ya'll made it! Nice!" He was doing his thing, and it was up to you to keep up. He was the perfect subject.

There was no way MTV was going to do a show with me. Networks order up a lot of experiments—like my five-minute reel on life with Maino—and reject most of them. That's the way this business runs. But I couldn't afford to waste a single minute.

After I submitted the five-minute DVD, which in my mind was a trailer to my feature documentary, an MTV exec called me to say, "This is pretty good!" as if it was the most surprising thing in the world.

"That's the goal," I said.

Snarkiness is one of my less attractive qualities.

MTV asked me to expand the reel to ten minutes, which was no problem because I had about two hundred hours of tape to work with. A couple of weeks later, I gave them the new version, and a few weeks after that, the same exec called again. "Pretty good," she said.

"Good," I replied, holding in at least four different snide comments.
"Why don't you make it fifteen minutes long?"
"All right."

This game went on until it was twenty-some odd minutes long and had surpassed "pretty good" and "good" to become "great."

Working hard, late at night, by myself. I have a weird thing about putting on a hoodie. Behind my head is that weird primitive storytelling diagram.

"We love this!" the exec said. "We can't believe it. I showed it to my boss, and he wants to come to your office to see how you work. You know, the whole operation that you have going."

Operation? I like that. I'm running an operation.

"Oh yeah, come to my office," I said from my "office," the filthy NYC apartment I shared with three other guys. "You're more than welcome. My door is open."

"Terrific. We'll be there next Friday at ten A.M."

I hung up and looked out the window.

That's awesome. MTV is coming to my office. I really need to find an office. What did I get myself into?

I thought about one of my friends' dad, an accountant in the Empire State Building, and how cool that'd be to invite them to my office on the seventy-third floor. But at ten A.M. his office would be filled with accountants, which wouldn't make any sense. I called everyone I knew, which was useless since most everyone I knew was still in college. Within an hour, it became clear: I wasn't going to find an office.

My small room, where the two execs sat on my bed.

"Listen, you're not going to believe this, but I don't think we can go to my office tomorrow morning," I told the exec over the phone. "I think it was a lady upstairs. There was a huge flood. You will not believe it. There's water up to my knees; I can't even move."

"Oh no. We're all very excited. We're coming!"

"No, you can't. There's water up to my waist now. It's getting worse and worse! You can't come here! You're going to get electrocuted and die!"

"We have to do something."

"I guess I can move all my editing equipment to my apartment and show you how I work here . . . I mean, there."

"Done."

Scanning my apartment, I saw empty beer cans strewn about a stained couch and grimy rug; old *New York Post*s and a few *Financial Times* layered over an ancient pizza box; piles of dirty clothes keeping the dust bunnies at bay. The idea of the people in charge of MTV coming to my apartment was horrifying. Really, really horrifying. But I got ready.

I cleaned up the whole place and ordered my roommates to stay in their rooms the next morning until the MTV people had left . . . no matter what. Then I called my unemployed friend, Troy, and said that if he came to the apartment at 9:30 A.M., wearing a suit and his hair gelled back (he loves doing that), and pretended to be my intern for an hour, I'd pay him twenty dollars (money saved from making *The Zen of Bobby V.*).

"Why would I do that?" Troy asked.

"Because it's twenty dollars."

So he came.

The next morning, with the place as clean as it was going to get, the MTV people arrived. Troy, doing a good imitation of a professional, brought them back to my tiny room, whose size instantly made things extraordinarily awkward. They had to sit on my bed while I showed them footage on my computer from my desk.

"What about this scene?" I said, muscling through the moment with aggressive cheerfulness. "Pretty cool, right?"

The execs, uneasily bouncing around my bed, were losing focus and starting to check out the pictures on the walls of my friends doing weird stuff and the eclectic reading material on my bedside table. Just then, thank God, Troy knocked on the door.

"So sorry to interrupt you guys," he said, speaking more slowly than usual and looking the two executives in the eye. "Just wanted to check in, make sure everyone's comfortable. Wanted to see if anybody needed some orange juice, coffee, doughnuts perhaps?"

What is he talking about? Orange juice and doughnuts? We hardly have water.

"We just came from breakfast," one of them said. "We're good."

I didn't breathe until ten minutes later when the MTV folks had left. It was a risky move, but one I'm glad I took, because in the end I turned those five minutes into a pilot that aired on September 13, 2010, to an audience of 4.8 million viewers—the highest-rated series launch in MTV's history. And I didn't show my abs once.

chapter eight

WHOSE WORLD IS IT ANYWAY?

ESPOLÓN ESPOLÓN
American

From "The Takeover": Flew to London for one night with poker player Nick Shulman. He gave me $40,000 to "hold on to." Couldn't watch the game, so I walked around the city with the green bag.

People started to worry that I forgot I was making an MTV show.

A homeless chick?

An autistic kid?

A *GQ* writer suggested I was making a public service announcement.

No. In doing a show, which had morphed from a full season of just Maino to one that featured underreported stories of kids going through rough times, I didn't want to feature cliché hardship. No model trying to make it in the big city. No group of friends trying to make it in Hollywood. But the real stuff that's happening to my generation. Mental illness and disabilities. Poverty. Abuse. Addiction. Artists. Activists. Students. Fighters. My plan was to tell engaging and substantive stories about important issues, masked as entertainment.

My obsessive need to do something right for this world comes from family dinners growing up.

When my dad wasn't traveling, he, my brother, my mom, and I would sit down for dinner. My mom, who admittedly hated to cook, specialized in chicken. A lot of it. But my dad couldn't even change a lightbulb, so we certainly didn't trust him in front of stoves and such.

Around the table, my dad would drink a shandy (beer and Sprite), my mom and brother water, and for me, a seltzer. I drank, and still do, tons of seltzer. And as Kramer from *Seinfeld* says, we'd "ask about how each other's days went." My mom talked about her work at the community health center in Peekskill. Her patients, mostly Ecuadorian immigrants with no health care, suffered real hardship. There was a young man with a serious heart condition but unable to afford treatment. Or the single mom who struggled to support her two sons back home in South America.

Then it was Dad's turn.

"Have to go to Norway and Sweden next week. There are some parliamentary hearings to review the effectiveness of aid and whether it is really getting to the poorest people in Africa."

From "Fifty Fists": Fighter Anthony Pettis breaks down in front of his father's gravesite.

Unaffordable cures, genocide. Lots of death and pain. All in one ordinary dinner conversation. These dinners defined who I am today. They made me aware that the world has many issues and that a meaningful life is about helping others.

We lived in a house where money was never talked about. There were no big-screen TVs or cable. That's not what mattered. Devoting your lives to others did. My mom did that one patient at a time, while my dad did it on a global scale. Anything else feels strange. I don't know if they'll ever know how much I love them for that.

Finding reality was a lot harder than I thought it would be. As soon as you say "MTV" and "show," every aspiring star and attention-seeker comes out to act crazy. The medium inherently made authenticity difficult. I was looking for survivors, not showboats.

I felt we had to feature one person with a mental disability, because it affects so many kids and continues to carry a large stigma in our society.

While filming in Harbor Place, I learned about the fine line between documenting lives and taking advantage of people. Toward the end of our stay at the assisted-living facility, one of our roommates, Dotty, passed away in a hospital room while we watched and filmed. She was shaking, going in and out of consciousness, and could hardly speak.

From "Froot Loops For Dinner": On subway after a long night with comedian Dan St. Germain

At the time, I questioned what side of the line we were on. It's a hard process to always get right. While in that hospital room, I went up to Dotty and told her I would kneel down and say a prayer. I didn't really know what I was going to say. I just got on a knee. Dotty leaned in and said, "Thank you." She knew what was going on more than anyone gave her credit for.

Following a person with special needs would also walk that fine line. Maybe for that reason, although we called a million different schools and institutions, no one would let us in. I didn't blame them for being protective. Yet again, it was Zinn's mom, Linda, who came to my rescue (she had also sent me Bobby V.'s email). She worked at a small school, a couple hours north of New York City, for kids with special needs. Linda has known me forever (she played a few roles in my home movies) and she knew that if we found an appropriate subject we'd really tell his story, not get him drunk and give him a rose. So she allowed us to interview the students to see if there was someone who could work.

Meeting Chad

Watching Chad, a 20-year-old man living with autism, during his five-minute interview on camera was so gripping that it was a pretty easy decision to pick him.

CHAD: My name's Chad. *(laughing)*

RESEARCH DIRECTOR: What really gets you pissed off?

CHAD: Celine Dion.

RESEARCH DIRECTOR: Why?

CHAD: Oh man, she just gives me a headache. . . . You know what else gives me a headache?

RESEARCH DIRECTOR: No.

CHAD: Not being treated like a man because I'm autistic. That makes me really mad.

From "The Street Queen": With Danielle, a homeless young woman that preferred the term "houseless." Other houseless friends and my crew nearby.

It got pretty hectic when my whole crew and I stormed into someone's life. Whether it was Nick, the youngest winner ever of the World Poker Tour, who battled chronic anxiety, or Dan, a young comic (and recovering alcoholic) prepping for the biggest show of his life, we bombarded them with mics, cameras, wires, walkie-talkies, and a crowd standing around.

But it was my job to make it feel like just another day. I would do my best to make sure while filming, our subjects could only see me, Jonah, Mike (the show's other cameraman), and Jon (my audio guy). I wanted them to think it was more of a home movie than an MTV show. On the last day, they could meet the entire team. But until then, it was too intimidating.

One of the hardest challenges I faced in season 1 was letting go. For my first two movies, I controlled every aspect. But when on the road filming, it's im-

possible to edit an episode, much less twelve episodes, all at the same time. So we hired five editors and five story editors who worked in five different editing rooms. For the first time, I wasn't scouring through hundreds of hours of footage by myself—which is what I was used to. Others would. Sure, I had final say and would come back with pages of notes on how to tell the story, but what if they missed a moment? What if they had terrible music taste? What if they got it all wrong?

I have a bad tendency to make last-second changes even after an episode is completed, or "locked."

When I was back in New York for a week here and there, I would spend eighteen hours or so in those edit bays, roaming from room to room. Sometimes, I was steaming. Even if a cut was good, I felt out of control.

They are screwing this all up.

Fix it, I would say.

Looking for a ride from California to Oregon

Hershel Simm's first game with his mom out of jail and watching in the stands

Coming out of tunnel as Anthony Pettis is announced at the Nationwide Arena in Columbus

Exploring Vegas

While filming on one of our first road trips, I read about other potential people to follow and how the edit was going.

I didn't know it yet, but it was time for me to grow up. I had to learn how to work with people. To trust other storytellers. And I couldn't be more grateful of the talent I was able to work with—and even more grateful for the hours they put in. A lot of times people say, "Well, what about MTV, did they control you?" No. The network was proud of the show. They would take my calls at three in the morning when I wasn't sure what to do, or let me come into their offices and plead for another couple days to let me edit an episode. When people talk about my show, the subjects aren't always the first thing that comes to mind. I think of all those people I have worked with who are just as committed to getting it right as I am. I'm very lucky.

I never met a subject before we started filming. I want the audience to be with me from the beginning.

I insisted on spending at least one week with my subjects, hanging out, eating, and sleeping at their place—and it was the sleeping part where I returned to what I do best. At night, after the rest of the crew returned to the hotel, it would be Jonah and me just like old times. That's often when we'd get our best stuff, because everyone's guard was down. On a car ride, Jonah filmed Hershel (a high school football star) and me talking about what it was like to be beaten with a belt as a child. We talked about what he wanted to say to his mom when she got out of jail. We spent nights in a San Francisco park with Danielle, a homeless teen known as "Heavy D," switching places to sleep because we knew cops were coming. I witnessed Chad walk circles around his house before tucking in for the night on a mattress on the floor of his parents' bedroom.

The #Originals

For one Saturday, I spent 12 straight hours with Tim (friend/editor) and Chris (friend/producer) editing two scenes. When we walked into the editing room, I opened my laptop and went on UStream.com. Quickly thousands of fans of the show were watching us edit. Just edit. They watched all day. We call them the #Originals.

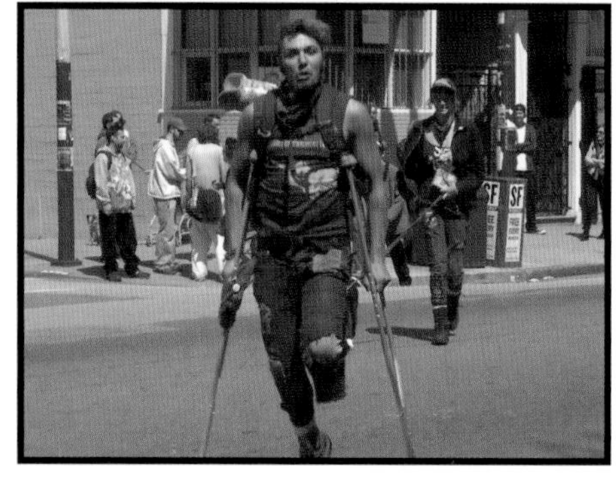

Working day and night didn't bother Jonah. He is relentless. "Jonah, did you get a shot of the speedometer?" one of the crewmembers joked while we were riding home in the car after wrapping a long week of shooting. Jonah didn't get it. Until he got it.

For the making of *The Zen of Bobby V.*, he filmed twelve hours straight, through rain and wind, while we climbed up Mount Fuji and back down (Bobby, an MLB manager, called it the most incredible athletic achievement he'd ever witnessed). It's great for the documentaries, but people can get really mad. If you throw up, he's there. Throw a punch, there he is. Break down crying? Yup. Jonah. There have been a few times that I had to stop him because he was going too far. When we are shooting, the world is his set. If he crosses the street while filming, and a cab is coming, he expects that cab to stop. Now, when walking in public areas, we have someone who monitors him.

I remember on an off day in Japan, Bobby was taking a casual stroll through a random city. Jonah, trying to get some shot, had the camera right up in Bobby's face. Bobby was mad, they had lost the night before, and so he suddenly stopped. He looked at Jonah and put his hand right up in front of the lens. "Does it always have to be right there?!" Bobby was pissed, I was scared, Jonah hadn't moved an inch . . . he was filming.

Jonah has used everything from helicopters to underwater cameras to get his shot. One-legged homeless guy chases Jonah down the street—they made up later.

Sleeping at comedian Dan St. Germain's apartment in New York City. Jonah to the left, me to the right. Jonah puts the camera on a tripod and keeps filming through the night—just in case something happens.

This is not a reality show. We don't know what is going to happen on any given day. There isn't a script. For me, the art of this kind of filmmaking is to be able to capture special moments in the blink of an eye—it may be a look, an expression, something as small as a grin—all of which connects the audience in a very special way; in a way that is unique. And when each day is done, I will look at Jonah and either say "we got it" or "we missed it." For me, reconciling being in the moment with worrying about how it will be edited is the hardest part.

Anytime I leave one of the people I've been following around for a week, I can never sleep that night. Guaranteed. I just know it. I no longer bother trying. It's the filmmaker's version of post-traumatic stress disorder. I have trouble assimilating into regular life for a while. I go through the motions, but am not at all there.

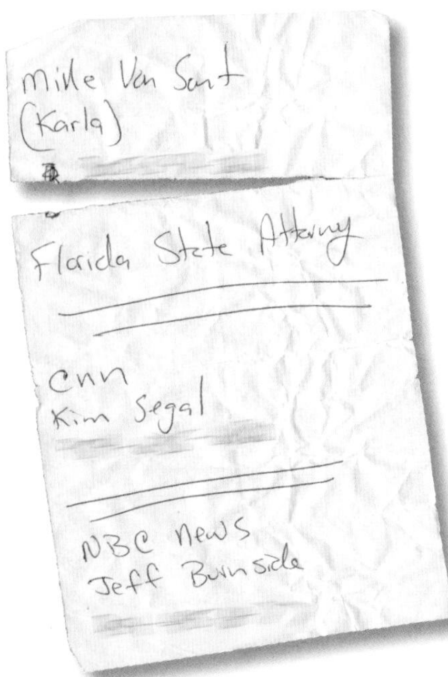
Mike Van Sant
(Karla)

Florida State Attorney

CNN
Kim Segal

NBC News
Jeff Burnside

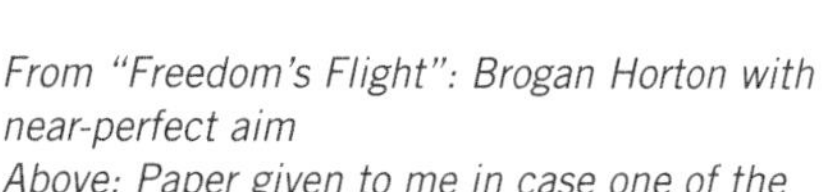
From "Freedom's Flight": Brogan Horton with near-perfect aim
Above: Paper given to me in case one of the other two were caught during mission

Imagine you've been living with a homeless girl for a week and today is the last day. You wake up in the morning after spending the night in the freezing cold on cardboard in a park. Then you walk around for half the day, asking passersby for change, like you've done for most of the week. But at one P.M. you know the crew is wrapping and the episode is over. Then it's time to say good-bye. You walk away, but the crew stays to de-mic her, and the moment is something you never forget. You are all alone.

After I said good-bye to Heavy D, I went to the parking lot, where I lay down on the asphalt before everyone else arrived.

Oh my God. I can't believe that just happened.

I needed to be alone, just as I had after I got the call from ESPN that they were going to make the Bobby V. movie. In times of big change, whether good or bad, I need a few moments to myself to understand before it gets tainted by real life.

Five hours later, I was back to real life, in a nice hotel room, taking a hot shower, and getting texts about going out with friends or "really" exploring San Francisco. My hamburger and fries arrived and I started to eat while watching TV. No ketchup. I called up room service and asked them to send up some. No problem.

But life was not entirely real yet, at least not my life. A part of me, if not all of me, was still back with Heavy D, right at that moment looking for a spot to sleep where she wouldn't get wet, or raped, or arrested.

Before I left Heavy D, people around me said I should give her money, try to get her an apartment or a job. "You can't just leave her there," they said. A lot of documentary filmmakers would argue that you capture their lives—and that's more or less it.

Talking with Heavy D on our last day together

Like a lot of kids, Heavy D, who'd been homeless since she was thirteen, had been let down by her entire world: her alcoholic parents, her school, other adults in her community. She had never experienced anyone asking her how her day was going or if she was safe. That is something everyone should have. So I gave Heavy D a cell phone with unlimited minutes. A tiny gift. But maybe the proudest one I've ever given.

"Call me anytime, at any point, and we can talk about anything you want," I said. "And if you don't call me, I am going to call you."

I walked around that night. Showered. Clean, shaven face. Clean clothes. Smelling fresh. On my way back from CVS, I called Heavy D. Like any normal friends, we talked about what was happening right then (she was drinking, I was buying a toothbrush) and how we'd stay in touch. But I avoided any mention of what was next for me. I felt terrible.

Every episode had its own movie poster and title, courtesy of my friend and coworker Bruce Jason Bohman.

WORLD OF JENKS
FIFTY FISTS
I GOT MY BROTHER MY MOM MY DAD MY COACHES I GOT ALL MY TEAMMATES ALL MY FRIENDS EVERYONE THERE IS SUPPORTING ME
EVERY TIME I PUNCH SOMEONE THATS LIKE FIFTY FISTS PUNCHING YOU IN THE HEAD" - PAT
WORLD OF JENKS
FREEDOM'S FLIGHT
Puppies Slaught
"IT'S JUST A RUSH, JUST AN ADRENALINE RUSH
THAT ANIMAL. IT'S ALL AROUND COLLECTIVE HAPPINESS THAT YOU CAN'T FIND ANYWHERE ELSE" - BROGAN
World of Jenks
THE TAKEOVER
"YOU MAKE $80,000 IN A DAY WHEN YOU'RE 17 DOING SOMETHING. WHO WOULDN'T CHASE THAT EVERYDAY?
IT'S NOT GOING TO BUY HAPPINESS AND NOT GOING TO TEACH YOU ANYTHING ABOUT THE WORLD." - NICK
10 20 30 40 50 40 30 20 10
HAIL MARY
World of Jenks
"SOMETIMES YOUR HEAD IS WRONG AND YOU HAVE TO FOLLOW THAT LITTLE VOICE IN YOUR HEART"-JESSI
FROOT LOOPS FOR DINNER
"ANYBODY WHO LOVES SOMETHING SO MUCH WILL FEEL THE MOST AT HOME DOING THAT THING.I COME INTO MY OWN SKIN, I LCAN LOSE MYSELF" - DAN
BLACK & GOLD
"I NEVER THOUGHT THAT I COULD HAVE AN IMPACT ON PEOPLE THE WAY I DO. IT'S UNBELIEVABLE. SOMETIMES I JUST WANT TO BREAK DOWN AND CRY. LITTLE KIDS THINK I'M A CELEBRITY. I'M JUST A HIGH SCHOOL FOOTBALL PLAYER. IT'S CRAZY I LOVE IT. THAT'S WHAT KEEPS ME GOING AND NOT GOING DOWN THE WRONG PATH." - HERSCHEL

Something I realized when going through footage: Nearly every subject looks at Jonah and Mike to shake their hand as we leave—the guys have been there for every moment also. As you can see, they continued to film with the other hand.

It's strange, because the moment I'm leaving, I have the biggest sense of relief. The intense seven-day experiment that I've been trapped inside of is finally over. But it's too late. I've fallen for my subjects so deeply, losing total track of everything else, including my family and friends; my subjects are stamped into my brain. After my experience with Heavy D, it was hard to eat. The food in my favorite restaurants was ruined by the thought of her picking through the garbage. Out drinking and watching sports at a bar, after my week with Chad, I winced every time one of my friends cursed. If I said one off-color remark around Chad, he talked about it almost nonstop for the rest of the day. His sensitivity rubbed off on me.

The whole show messes with my head, which I kind of like. After the first season of *World of Jenks*, I was profoundly humbled. Yes, I exude confidence that can border on arrogance. But my experience of living with all these different people has made me aware of the fragility of the structures that hold up our sense of self.

In the middle of that first season, I was out at a club, where I ran into some reality TV star. After the introductions were made, he asked me "So what do you get?"

"Excuse me?" I said, not sure of his meaning.

"What are your ratings?"

What an absurd way to identify yourself. I could make fun of the reality star endlessly, but I get it. In a way, we all do that—understand our value in terms of external factors like the clothes we wear, the neighborhood we live in, the school we attend, the ratings our show gets.

Making my show has taught me how quickly all that is broken down. A week is a short time, but it's enough to eradicate anything you hold on to. In seven days of being homeless in San Francisco, gambling in Las Vegas, going undercover to expose horse-slaughter farms in Miami, I am no longer Andrew Jenks who lives in his own Manhattan apartment, has a staff of thirty-five, goes to Knicks games, and hangs out in bars. All of that's gone. Really gone.

When those barriers are broken, what's left is a startling and beautiful fact: Everyone's story is important and unique.

chapter nine
YO, JENKS

PRESIDENT
BILL CLINTON

It is the night of the 2012 VMAs—the hottest awards show on the planet. However, this time around my show isn't airing afterward, and I am nowhere near Los Angeles.

I am across the country, watching the President of the United States speak to millions of Americans at the Democratic National Convention in Charlotte, North Carolina. Sitting in MTV's media booth, overlooking the entire stadium with Scarlett Johansson, Anderson Cooper, Caroline Kennedy, Bill Clinton, and more important, twenty thousand people celebrating the accomplishments of their beloved president—it's all very surreal.

After shooting season 1 of *World of Jenks*, I convinced the MTV brass to let me cover the presidential election. They eventually agreed—allowing me to take on the role of MTV's "correspondent." I had lobbied hard for the job. "You never would have gotten this if you hadn't kept bugging us about it," said one MTV vice president. Now I am watching President Barack Obama give one of the biggest speeches of his life. I was on the floor as President Clinton gave his speech just a day earlier. I was also on a panel with Chelsea Clinton—as *she* interviewed *me* about what I've heard from young people across the country. But it wasn't just being in charge of covering the election that I had to convince MTV about.

At the president's convention speech

2012 DEMOCRATIC
FLORIDA
GEORGIA

LOUISIANA

Roaming around before Governor Mitt Romney's speech

In season 2 of *World of Jenks*, I wanted the show to be an hour long. And I only wanted to follow 1–3 subjects for an entire year. It would give me more time to get to know the people. For season 1, thirty minutes every week with a different person in every episode didn't give the viewers a chance to really get to know anyone. MTV wasn't so sure. So for two weeks, I sat down with an assistant editor and edited four different subjects together from season 1 into an hour-long episode. We weaved all four characters in and out of every act. It's called a proof of concept (POC). So this assistant editor and I sat in a small, dark room trying to prove to the network that there was a better version of the show that could be made. I thought of when I'd edited the Maino episode by myself in that old, crummy apartment. And then I thought of the staff of nearly a hundred people that worked on season 1. And now here I was, back in a small, dark room with an editor I had just met—trying to convince an entire network that there was a better way of doing things.

Fake it till you make it. Don't hear no. Adapt.

Turns out MTV had a similar idea—so I guess I didn't need to do that much convincing in the first place anyway.

While filming season 2, I was seated on a plane waiting to head to Oakland to shoot with a subject, when another subject we were following, Kaylin, texted me. Kaylin had two different types of cancer, one of which is known to come back within a few years, and both of which have left her in chronic pain for life. She says she will be "very lucky" if she makes it to forty. Every day is a battle for her. A life I could never imagine.

Footage from an iPhone as Kaylin and I wait in the ER

"I am not feeling well," her simple text read.

Kaylin never texts me—never about all the pain she feels on a daily basis, never about boy troubles, never about anything other than she's not feeling well enough to film (which is why we gave her a camera to self-record how she feels on days she just can't even deal with talking).

Once I got that text, I jumped off the plane.

"It's too late, sir," said a steward.

"I don't care," I responded, in a moment of urgency and trepidation.

I got into a cab and headed to the emergency room. As I rode to the ER, I called the only person I knew would have the passion to get there sooner than I: Jonah. "Bring your iPhone," I told him. "And make sure it has plenty of space." I knew it was illegal to film in a hospital—especially when you haven't told anyone you plan on doing so. To troubleshoot that, I called in Jonah and another coworker, Kassie, in the middle of the night. When you have a crew that believes in you, that believes in your project, a phone call to meet at the ER at three in the morning comes with the job. It comes with our line of work. And it's what makes it a special bond between people that really believe their collective work can change lives.

Kaylin at a "trunk show'"in New York City

Kaylin was already there when I arrived. As we sat for hours wondering if the cancer was back, I asked her how she was feeling.

"I am worried about tomorrow."

"The scans? What they might say?"

She looked at me like I was an idiot.

"No, I have a job interview tomorrow. I want to make it."

I couldn't believe that at that moment she was worried about a job interview.

After filming Chad, a young man with autism, for season 1, I thought his story was too good to not continue telling. I went back and filmed more to convince MTV to bring him back for all of season 2.

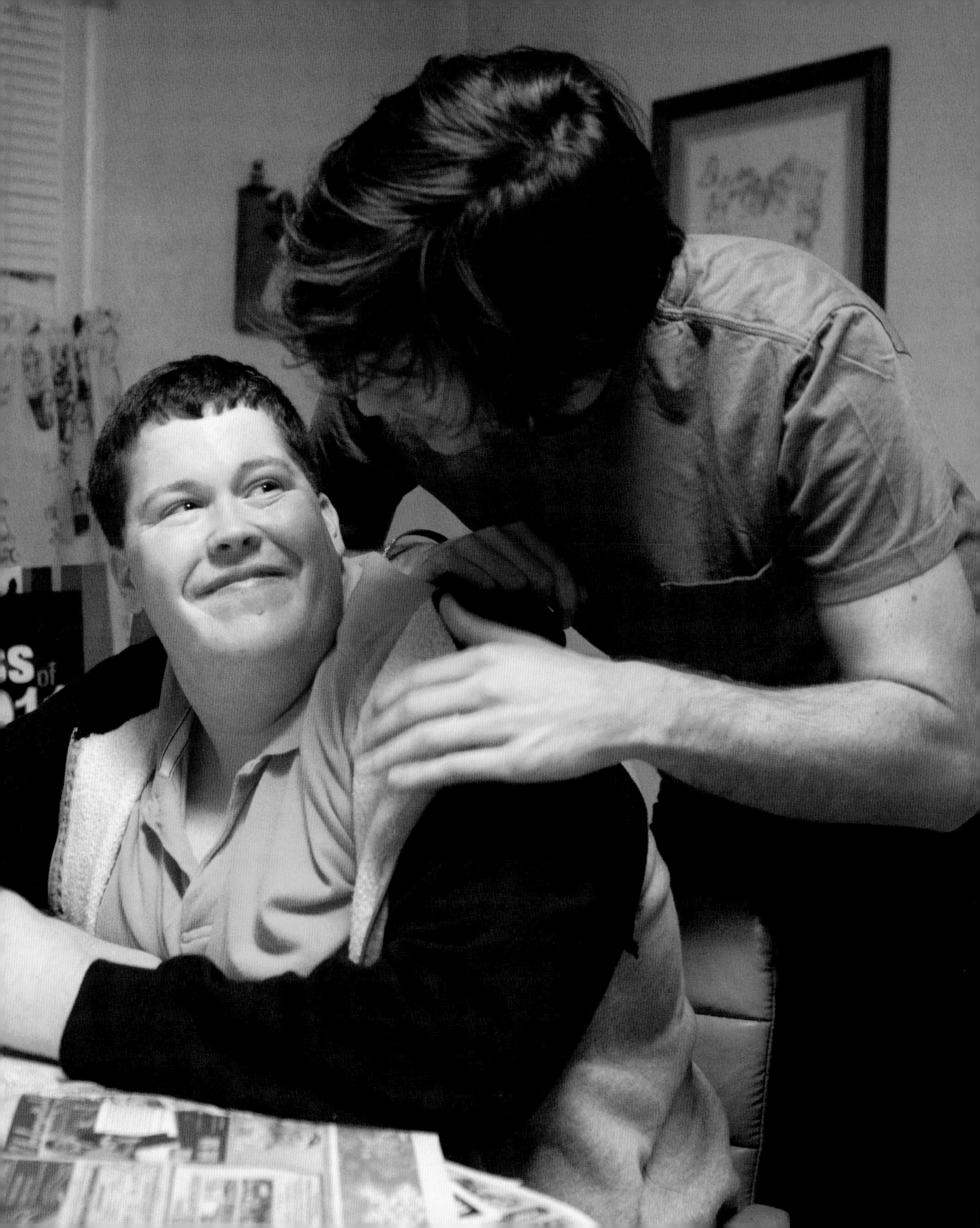

Our 3-camera setup in the car. Chad and I would drive 90 minutes to school each way. With most people I've followed, you spend a lot of time the car.

Other than trying to be a friend, I make sure I get the entire night filmed. After all, that's my job, too—and how I got there in the first place.

With two iPhones, Kassie and Jonah pretended to play video games but actually sat there and filmed the entire thing. Kassie in one corner, Jonah in the other. Nobody in the room knew it, but we had multiple angles to cut back and forth with. The editor was quite happy. Technology has truly changed the art of documentary film.

Kaylin, as I write this, is "okay"—still in chronic pain, but able to get up in the morning and work at a fashion company in New York City (yes, she did get that job). And so my life, crisscrossing the country, continues.

Now, as I write this last chapter, I am back in my Charlotte hotel room, watching the footage we shot of my commentary right before the president took the stage. I watch the reruns on cable, tying to dissect what the president said compared to what Governor Romney said.

When I ask presidential candidates questions, I always get a call from Matt: "That was really pathetic, Andrew. You really going to let him off that easy? Damn."

He is sincere in his convictions. And he is almost always right.

He never accepts anything less than what I can be—and that's the best brother anyone can have.

The Crew

I went from a guy editing alone in his bedroom with a fake intern whom I actually had to pay to a guy in charge of a big staff. Now this was an operation:

3 Executive Producers
2 Supervising Producers
1 Line Producer
2 Associate Producers
1 Production Manager
1 Production Coordinator
2 Office Assistants
1 Field Producer
1 Audio Guy

3 Story Editors
5 Editors
2 Production Assistants
2 Directors of Cinematography
1 Assistant Cameraman
1 Media Manager
1 Research Director
4 Researchers

1 Supervising Postproduction Manager
1 Production Manager Assitant
1 Music Supervisor
1 Assistant Music Supervisor
Endless Lawyers
An incredible group from "the network," MTV
You get the point

Season 2, with D-Real, remembering his brother

Eventually, I shut off the TV. I can't take it anymore.

The process of electing the president of the United States is very ordinary, even though what's at stake is anything but. I've been struck by the fact that there is not the same urgency on the campaign trail as with the people I follow every day for my show. For my subjects, decisions feel like, and sometimes are, life or death. The candidates' need to do something is nowhere near as pressing.

As I stare at the ceiling, I am thinking of my room in New York City. I have no rug, nothing on the walls, and a fridge that hasn't worked in months—I wonder if I still haven't thrown out that old Chinese takeout. Must have smelled up the whole kitchen by now. There is a bed, a dusty television, and a couch with tags still on it. For someone who hated sleeping away from home, I now know the room layouts of Hilton hotels more than my own apartment.

. . . and a few friends' couches.

I realize I am not going to be sleeping. No fan. Too much on my mind. Some things never change. It sucks, but "so it goes." In between seasons 1 and 2 I went on a college speaking tour—thirty colleges in two months. From the University of Southern California to the University of Nebraska to Nassau Community College to the University of Nevada–Las Vegas. You name it, I've probably been there—or somewhere close.

Because I appear on TV trying to understand other people's lives, a lot of people who don't know me trust me. "Yo, Jenks," they always begin. "You should do a show about this . . ." After I'm done with my talks at the colleges I visit, I speak one-on-one with hundreds of students who come up and tell me things they may not tell another stranger. Parents dying. Overwhelming insecurity. Disabilities. Mistakes that seem irreparable. *Yo, Jenks.*

Speaking at colleges across the country. It's a fun challenge. All I have is a mic and 90 minutes to tell stories and keep the audience entertained.

Every time I think I've heard it all, I hear something new.

And for those stories that aren't handed to me on a piece of paper, I jot down many of them on my laptop. I like to jot them down—I just don't want to forget. As I walked around in my Charlotte hotel room only an hour or two after the president spoke, I remembered Freddy, a guy my age whom I had met at the University of North Carolina a few months back. He couldn't afford college but drove two hours to hear me speak, and found a way to

get into the hall even though he wasn't a student. Afterward, Freddy waited on line, and then told me quite a few things before handing me a note. It talked about how he takes care of his deaf mother. How he tries to take care of his four kids with three different women (he certainly isn't perfect). His minimum-wage job. His dad, whom he loved but was a drug addict and got shot six times—now dead. After lying in bed and realizing I won't be sleeping in Charlotte, I put on shorts and a T-shirt, text a producer for the car keys, and get in our Hertz van and drive. I call Freddy and let him know I am on my way. He knew I was in town and said he'd meet me if I called him at any point. He wasn't looking for pity, just a witness to his life.

His neighborhood is nothing like the beautiful convention hall I had attended hours earlier. No balloons floating from the ceiling, no police presence, certainly no hope. The area he lives in is poor—and very violent. We talk for two hours in my rented car—his apartment was recently shot at and it's safer driving around. We don't talk about how to save the world—for now, that's too much. We talk about movies, music, and for most of the time, how he can best take care of his kids moving forward. How they can get a decent education, enjoy the small things in life, and, quite literally, live to be eighteen years old and have a shot at college. I give Freddy some gifts I picked up at the convention, and some money for him to buy his kids some books (although I joke that we both know the money will go to his kids' new shoes). I remind Freddy that one day, when he makes it big, he can buy me a new pair of Air Jordans. He looks at me and smiles. Both of us hope to death that this can become a reality—but neither of us are naïve enough to think it's a sure thing. Getting out of the ghetto is no easy task.

I return to my hotel room at four A.M.

Down the road, when I think of what to ask President Obama or Governor Romney, I don't think about how nearly 50 percent of Millennials are unemployed or that most of us are $25,000 in debt after leaving college. I don't think about the endless statistics that I have come to memorize.

I think about Freddy. I think about Kaylin. I think of all the faces I've seen and all the stories I've heard.

When I cover the candidates, I feel the pressure of those stories. Representing young people disenfranchised from politics, I feel a very real and deep responsibility to tell their stories. That's why I don't like it when people call me a reporter; I'm a conduit.

But you can't tell their stories unless you've connected with them. And earned their trust.

Everyone has different priorities and value systems, but it's always important to show that you get it, that you are willing to act on what you believe in and give something in return. Trust. During my week with Maino, he took me to the massive, crumbling housing projects in Bedford-Stuyvesant, Brooklyn, where he'd grown up. Without making a single phone call, we found ourselves in a stairwell with twenty other guys, as if Maino had a hidden radar system to let them know he was in the 'hood.

"Yo, we're going to do Jenks up," he said in the gloomy stairwell, gang members surrounding me. "We're going to do him up."
Then everyone started in, "Yeah. We're going to do Jenks up. We're going to do Jenks up."

I had no idea what they were talking about. I got real nervous as they got louder and louder until they were yelling it: "Yo! We're going to do Jenks up! We're going to do him up!"

"All right. Let's go," Maino said.
"Yeah. Do me up," I said, still unsure of what he meant or why we were in this stairwell. "Here we go."

I looked over to my left, and there were two guys, rolling these really fat blunts. At first I thought I only saw two, but then I realized it was more or less one for everyone. Maino looks over at me and says it more softly now, "We're going to do you up."

Oh, no way.

"What?"
"You want to roll? You gotta roll."

I can only imagine what I was yapping about in a stairwell with all of Maino's buddies.

It was one in the afternoon on our second day of shooting for this show that I had just been given fifty grand by MTV to make. And he wanted to get me high?

The blunts were being passed around in slow motion until eventually one arrived at me. You could see everyone's eyes slowly turn to rest on me—even Jonah, who was giving me an expression that I knew well: *Dude, are you really going to do it?* He knew the repercussions.

But I took a hit to show everyone that I could take a hit.

"Come on, fellas. I can roll. Please." I handed it to Maino. "You see, my man? I'm good."

"Pff. Man, you kidding?" he said, pushing away the blunt. "I don't mess around with drugs."

Room 335:

91-minute movie, 210 hours of footage

The Zen of Bobby V.:

83-minute movie, 550 hours of footage

World of Jenks Season 1:

19-minute-and-20-second episode, on average 130 hours of footage each

World of Jenks Season 2:

42-minute episode, over 1,500 hours of footage shot

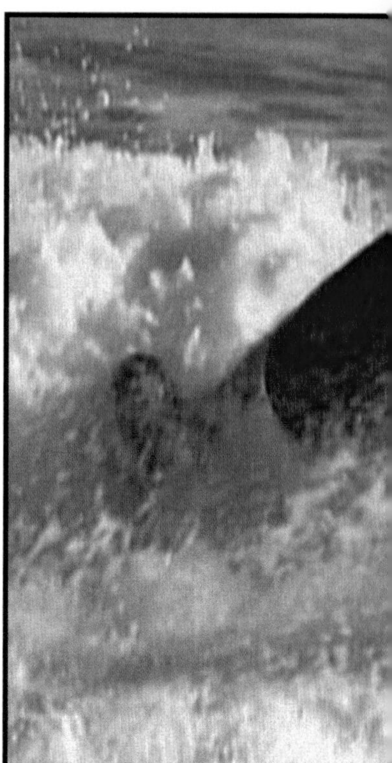

While Maino walked away, leaving me with these guys for an hour in the stairwell, I realized an important lesson that I'd learn over and over again:

There is always a test to pass before people will trust you.

With the mixed martial artist Anthony Pettis, the first thing he did was put me in the ring to see if I'd fight someone. I did, and I herniated a freakin' disk.

When I met pro surfer Anastasia Ashley, the first thing we did was surf. But not little waves so that we could get funny shots of me falling off and her laughing. No, she put me in water where I literally had a panic attack and almost drowned.

When I was with Heavy D, she gave me a choice, "Are you going to sleep out here on the street, or are you going to go to a hotel room tonight?"

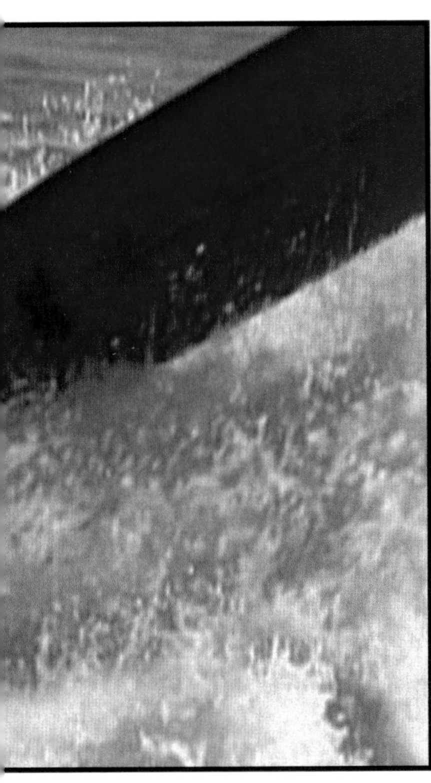
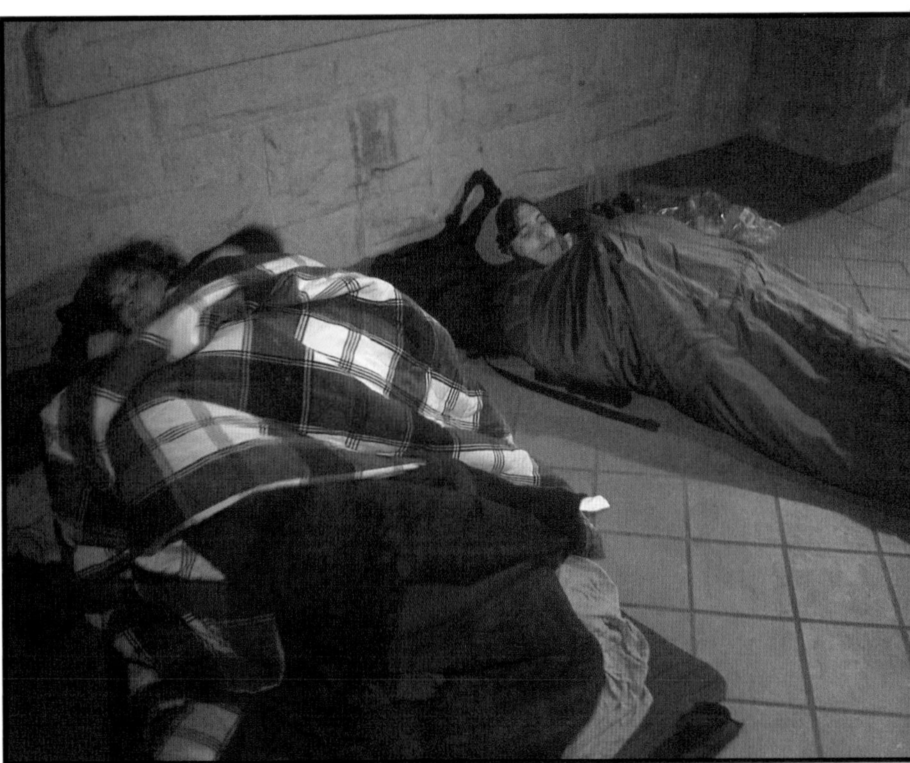

Bobby V. wanted to know we were learning a word a day of Japanese and that we were the first ones in the stadium and the last ones out.

Even in the nursing home, the residents eyed us suspiciously until we sat down *on time* to eat four P.M. dinner and *competitively* play six P.M. bingo.

Whenever I face a hard moment—from pitching a new idea to a roomful of network executives, to standing up for a friend like Heavy D by calling out her alcoholic parents on their lies—I remind myself there are only two choices: You can show up or not. No matter how hard that moment is, you have to ask, will you be kicking yourself for the rest of your life if you don't do it? You have to trust yourself.

My biggest dream, the one I've had since my parents let me use that camera while living in Belgium, is to shoot a feature film. I've written a script that I am waiting to direct when the time is right. I just returned from a trip to Los Angeles for a few weeks listening to producers and agents give me a list of reasons as to why this movie can't be made. Nothing new. Nothing that I haven't heard before.

Other than loyalty, the one trait that I feel like has gotten me this far—far enough to write a book about my adventures—is putting in the time. Working hard. I mean *really hard*. A lot of people think I have a TV show because I was in the right place at the right time (which I was) or because I'm good-looking (debatable). Even if I'm the luckiest person in the world (I am), I pride myself on outworking everyone, by not stopping until I've grabbed every last bite of material.

Courtside at the Knicks game

The reward for all this work isn't fame, although some of the perks are pretty nice, particularly free Knicks tickets. One of my proudest moments was taking my brother to Madison Square Garden, where we were used to the last section, the back row, and bringing him down to our $2,000 pair of front-row seats (that we didn't have to pay for) where our feet touched the court and we listened to the players talk trash.

But fame is fleeting.

Above: On the phone with D-Real while filming with Kaylin. I stay in touch with everyone as much as posssible.
Below: En route to the beach with Chad, the car breaks down. Jonah starts filming highway for no reason.

The guy I wouldn't be here without: Jonah

JALAR
CUBIERTA
Weight of hatch:
15kg
approx. 33lbs
Emergency
opening
Salida
de emergencia

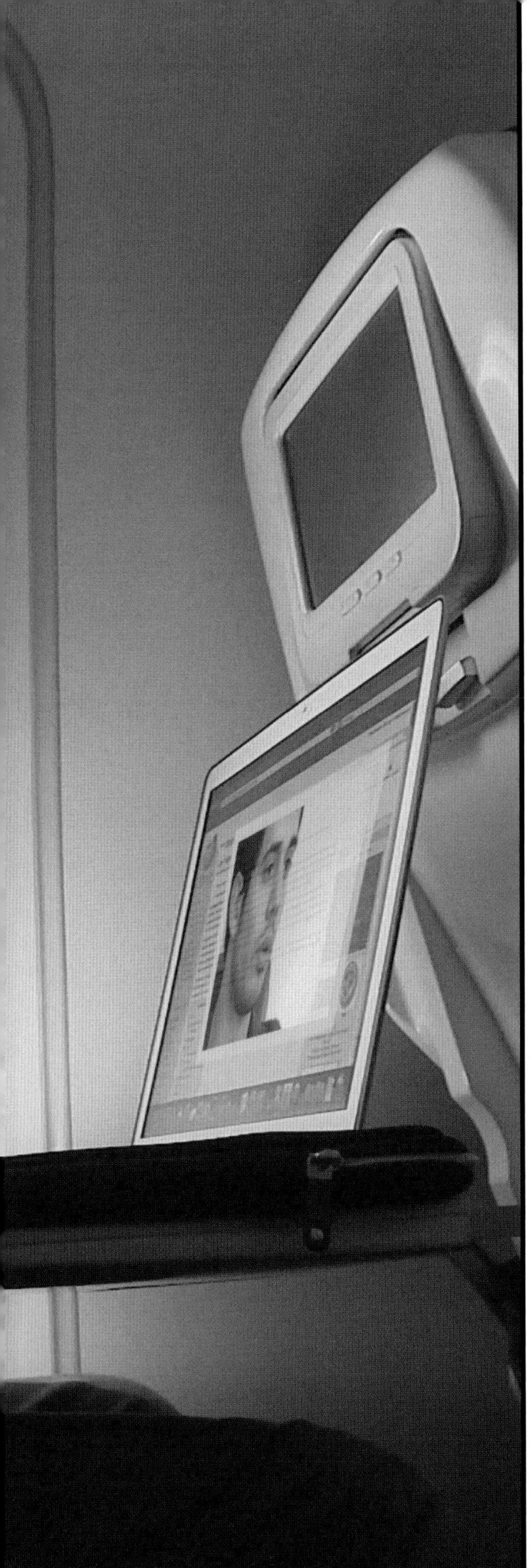

When I went to the MTV Movie Awards (only because J.J. said he'd come with me, and he only came because we got to live the life for a weekend with a free Navigator, room at the fancy L'Hermitage Hotel, and box seats for game 1 of the NBA finals of the Lakers against the Celtics), I quickly realized I really didn't need to be there at all. Months before, while my show was still on the air, I had done an event and the paparazzi had shouted for me to move into their frame. "Yo, Jenks, move into my world," they yelled, snapping my picture. This time, with my show in between seasons, while I walked the red carpet, I could hear them asking, "Who's he?"

Crickets.

No, the reward for working hard is getting to do more work. And better work. "Work" is a word I use so other people will understand what I'm talking about, but I don't think about it that way. For me, putting the world down on film is living. Giving people a voice.

I'm finally getting sleepy as I return to my hotel room at four A.M. I have two more hours until it's on to another plane, another college, another presidential speech, another day of filming, or if I am lucky, a chance to see Mom, Dad, and Matt.

Acknowledgments

Mom, Dad, and Matt—The strongest family one could ask for. I love you all so much. I am so incredibly lucky. **J.J., Nana, Grandad, and Wilfred**—For leaving me unique and incredible outlooks on life. **Beth, David, Alex, and Nicholas**—You always make me laugh. Thanksgiving dinners, ski trips, N's college graduation. **Craig**—Showing me the best books to inspire new projects. **Pebbles**—I wish I was there for you more. Anyone who has come through the **Hill Household**—If I went through every friend and every parent from The Manor, there would have to be another version of this book. Your support is truly special. **Jonah Quickmire Pettigrew**—I would not be here without you. Thank you for being such a good friend.

The Scholastic Team. **Rick DeMonico**—Designing the best book I could have ever imagined. A dream to work with. So much talent—I really don't know how you did it. **Rebecca Paley**—Able to make sense of my words. Incredible writer. This book doesn't exist without you. Thank you for putting in the time to understand me. **Brenda Murray**—Sticking with me when I missed every deadline. All while having a child :) **Debra Dorfman**—Bringing me into the Scholastic doors. Letting me tell my story and not having to change my voice. **Paul Banks**—We did it! Look at the cover!

John Hoffman and the HBO Team—For reading that *Variety* review and believing in the film.

Dan Silver, John Dahl, Conner Shell, and ESPN Team—For giving 3 shabby guys the money to get an opportunity of a lifetime. **Larry Rocca**—For making us laugh and showing us the way in Japan.

Brooke Posch—I have never met someone so loyal and so caring. For being the best network exec and far more importantly, the best friend anyone could ever ask for. You're the funniest and smartest person I know. **Brent Haynes**—Taking a chance on me. Letting me tell stories that we both believed in. **Chris Mirglinai**—"Eh, didn't think the pilot was as good as I had heard." From there on out, you have been my go-to for everything. Not sure I'd be able to get through a day without your talent and will. A great friend. **Chris Linn, Tony DiSanto David Janollari, and the MTV Team**—For giving us the support and backing to make our show a success. **David Snyder**—The definition of someone who never falls short of perfect. **Michelle Shieffen**—Master of story. Master of putting your heart into something. And master of arguing with me for all the right reasons. **Mike Sierakowski**—I am ready for your "Badlands"! **Adam Lublin**—For introducing me to Maino. Putting in so many hard hours from the very beginning. **The WOJ Team**—Relentless. From pre, to production, to post. I am upset I can't name you all, because there is a mountain of talent, work ethic, and sincere love.

Cheri Quickmire and David Pettigrew—For your endless support. **Will Godel**—So lucky I met you freshman year. Never forget *West Wing* eps. And a big thank you to your wonderful Parents. **Andrew Muscato**—For working so hard with Bobby V., even the stuff that never happened, Glen Mills! **Tom Oliva**—Putting your heart into our film festival. **ID-PR team (Sheri and Annick), Joel McKuin, David Levin, Brian Greenberg, Andy Roth, Christina Kuo, Tom Young, Andy Elkin, Adam Berkowtiz, Lauren Schwartz, Lauren Auslander, Matt Rosen**—For putting in the time to give me a shot at success. All of those friends and coworkers I haven't been able to mention, I am forever grateful for the role you played in my life. **You know who you are.**

Lastly, to all of those who have given me a chance to take a peek inside your lives. Thank you for taking a chance. You ultimately gave me a voice.